Adjustment and Life Satisfaction of Middle Aged Couples

Adjustment and Life Satisfaction of Middle Aged Couples

Dr. Shweta Nema

KALPAZ

First Published, 2019

Published by

Kalpaz Publications
C-30, Satyawati Nagar,
Delhi – 110052
Ph.: 011-47034999, 9811692060
www.kalpazpublications.com
E-mail: kalpaz@hotmail.com

Printed at: G. Print Process, Delhi

Cataloging in Publication Data—DK
Courtesy: D.K. Agencies (P) Ltd. <docinfo@dkagencies.com>

Nema, Shweta, author.
Adjustment and life satisfaction of middle aged couples / by Dr. Shweta Nema.
pages cm
Study conducted in Narsimhapur District of Madhya Pradesh, India.
Includes bibliographical references.
ISBN 9789353240196

1. Middle-aged persons—India—Narsimhapur (District)—Psychology. 2. Married people—India—Narsimhapur (District)—Psychology. 3. Adjustment (Psychology)—India—Narsimhapur (District) 4. Satisfaction. I. Title.

LCC HQ1059.5.I4N46 2018 | DDC 305.24409543 23

Contents

Acknowledgement 7

1. Introduction 9
2. Review of Literature 19
3. Research Methodology 33
4. Result and Discussion 41
5. Summary, Conclusion and Suggestions 77

Bibliography 91

Index 99

Acknowledgement

Many thanks to Dr. Indu Bansal and Dr. Suvidha, my thesis chair, for all their help and support in the process of writing my thesis. Their kind advice and guidance has greatly contributed to this being an exciting and rewarding experience. Thanks to my father, Mr. Sunder Lal Nema and my mother Mrs. Suman Nema, whose support, financially and emotionally, has made this possible and encouraging me. My brothers Saurabh and Saket, their insight and counsel have been extremely valuable. There are so many wonderful people who have made this process possible and rewarding. I cannot say enough to express my sincere gratitude for all of their support. Thank you to my friends.

Finally, I would like to thank all the people who participated in my research. Everyone who gave me their time and information is greatly appreciated. An additional thanks goes to those who responded in my survey.

Dr. Shweta Nema

Chapter - 1

Introduction

Theoretical Background

Middle Age

Middle Age (also called midlife, middle adulthood), part of life between young and old age, is difficult to define in generalities, since there are variations in attitudes and behaviors at this point. The boundaries of midlife are fuzzy, with no clear demarcation. According to Collin's Dictionary, Middle age is usually considered to occur approximately between the age of 40 and 60. While prominent social scientist, Erik Erikson, sees it ending a little later and defines middle adulthood as between 40 and 65. Middle adulthood begins with a transition (40-45), followed by a life structure (45-50). This structure is re-evaluated (50-55) and ends in a culminating life structure (55-60). Those between ages of 40 (modal entry years) and 60 (when old age begins) are typically considered as middle aged, but there is at least a 10 years range on either end, so that it is not uncommon for someone to consider middle age to begin at 30 and end at 75 (Lachman, 2001).

In the age group of 40 and 60 years, adult find as much changes in their lives as they did when they were younger, and as they will when they are older. Indeed, it is the transitions to various stages (e.g., the return to work, the "empty nest", care giving) triggered by the occurrence of life events in the domains of work and the family (e.g., re-entry into the paid labour force, adult children leaving home, care for aging parents).

Middle age is characterized by competence, maturity, responsibility and stability and also the time of transference of authority, freedom and decision taking power to next generation. Middle age is a phase of transition when life patterns are revised in several ways to adapt to the new lifestyle. People at this stage want to enjoy the success of job, satisfaction derived from the family and social life as well as look forward to the success of their children, aging parents, the use of leisure time and plan for old age. This is the phase when people face entirely new set of challenges, expectations and liabilities and have to make several compromises. There may be many other aspects of life where one has to adapt to the changes like parenthood crises, coping with the untimely death of the spouse, etc. The occurrences of physical changes lead to changes in behavior also.

Middle life is a period of higher fulfillment, better health, more authority and greater financial stability than any other stage of life. There are physical and psychosocial changes associated with this time period that is different for women and for men. In the middle life men and women start believing in mortality (ushered in by body sensations, major illnesses, or death of parent) coupled with an acceptance of the shrinkage of possibilities for the future. It is generally considered to result from recognition that future possibilities have diminished and all goals and dreams set earlier in life will not be met. There is often a shift in roles between women and men in middle life called the midlife cross-over that strongly affects marriage. At middle age, there is a direct reversal as women come into their own with greater importance placed on work/career and personal goals and men become more aware or more needful of intimacy.

People have made consistent choices in certain directions and they often don't feel much freedom to significantly change their lives. People who feel disappointed and dissatisfied about their lives tend to feel less optimistic, in this age. Marital relationship shifts: from the more romantic, idealistic, and/or sexual emphasis, through the more prosaic, child-rearing, team-mate era. These previous sequences might have culminated in a relationship that is seasoned, stable and more satisfactory or more conflictual, tenuous and alienated than at any other time. In the absence of children, the conjugal bond, whatever its nature, will gain prominence. Others focus on mortality, become attached to the idea that more time has gone by than remains, see the beginnings of physical decline, and feel stress at the fact that they are not where they want to be in life. This stress may lead to actual grief and depression.

Middle Age Adjustments

It is important to adjust naturally with the transitions that occur both physically and mentally. At this stage it is good to look at the world with new perspective and changed interests. Some may find this stage really difficult and hard to cope with. Following are some of the important changes faced in middle age.

The age of physical changes

The period of middle age is typically marked with physical changes. Loss and graying of hair, joint pain, osteoarthritis, osteoporosis, sagging muscles, appearance of wrinkles etc. are common phenomenon. These changes are natural and add to graceful ageing and soberness of personality. The body system functions start to deteriorate in many, the people at this age may feel weak, have gastro -intestinal problems, suffer from insomnia, feel fatigue quite frequently, may have aches and pains, dental caries. Although with better medical and nutritional benefits of progressive societies, people feel much connected and youthful than in the past. In addition to age-related physiological changes, few events as change of work, change of place, death of a spouse, serious illness of spouse may also alter physical health and responsibilities.

These may aggravate emotional stress, physical fatigue, financial strain common difficulties associated with caring for a spouse at home are etc. Nevertheless, husbands and wives accept the responsibility for care giving when necessary, deal positively with the demands.

Changes occur in the physiological and reproductive functioning, virility and fertility of individuals. Loss of sex drive and sexual attractiveness may lead to stress, conflict and depression in some people. People without intimate relationship at this stage of life may manifest mood swings, self-criticism, carelessness towards business, hostility. Some people develop interest in cultural activities for example: attend concerts, lectures, religious programs, reading, writing, painting, social work and so on.

Intimacy and behavioral changes

Intimacy and sexual satisfaction relate to marital satisfaction and stability. Continued positive interaction lower rate of mental illness and likely hood to live longer. Relationship satisfaction in men depend on health, physical intimacy and sexual functioning, while in women only sexual functioning predicts relationship satisfaction. Intimate relationship such as touching, talking and feeling of togetherness also helps mid-age individual in emotional well-being.

The second most frequent period for divorce is at midlife after during the first 4-7 years of a marriage. Divorce is often linked to infidelity with

60-70% of men and 20-30% of women. There is also high rate of remarriage in midlife, especially among men.

Changes in family relations and adjustment

Chronic marital conflict at this stage may take the form of either hot arguments or silent distance. The spouses need to be closer in relationship with one another but marriage for certain families is synonymous with conflict. It is more difficult to cope up with the 'empty nest' period. For some this may be a traumatic time when domestic responsibilities get minimized and one may find life monotonous, when there is no family oriented activity to perform.

The period of middle age is typically marked with new responsibilities of caring for younger children and grandchildren, and sometimes older parents needing more attention and extra assistance. People at this stage also have to prepare for their own retirement.

Financial adjustments

The expenses on medical facilities for parents, college fees for children, mortgage on house, expenses on social events arrange expenses for marriage of children and other family expenses become high during middle adulthood. In case of dual employment the gross family income is larger and the expenses can be met in better manner. But in case of single employment all financial burden goes to the working spouse. Because of high demands on expenditure, mid-adults feel like on a treadmill one can never get off.

For some adults who are well established and at the peak of career and planned funds for retirement this period is very smooth easy and satisfactory. But for others who have ups and downs in their career and haven‘t well-established this time can be real challenging and painful.

Emotional adjustment

Emotional behaviors expressed by couples differed as a function of age, gender, and marital satisfaction (Carstensen et al., 1995). Mid-age couples become more realistic and practical about their relation and family issues.

The intensity of the middle-age intimacy crisis depends on the need satisfaction of the relationship and the success achieved in the previous stages of intimacy. Older adults are put more emphasis or positive aspects of close relationships and emotionally positive and responsive listening to successful conflict resolution.

Positive and negative affect represent spontaneous, ongoing emotional reactions to every day experience. Children generate more daily problems and worries but also more fun and enjoyment.

Carl Jung described the developmental task of the second half of life as the need to develop neglected inner resources and enrich the inner life which may result in the impoverishment of the inner life – the world of feelings, values and inner creativity. Failure to accept the changes may lead to serious traumatic situations like mental illness, use of drugs, addiction problems, alcoholism and at times suicide or homicide.

Marital adjustment

In typical Indian families, husband is expected to provide protection to the family and he is considered as head of family; while wife is expected to make home and strong companion, upon whom the husband can rely.

But sometimes this leads for unsatisfactory relationship due to feeling of lack of time to interact freely with husband and provide adequate love and care for their children. The other reason may be physical and mental exhaustion due to heavy and never ending work, indifferent attitudes of family members.

Life satisfaction

Life satisfaction examined from the perspective of subjective well-being refers to people's own evaluation of their lives. For middle-aged individuals life satisfaction is shaped by satisfaction with one's work, family life, health and daily state of affairs and of U shaped.

As mentioned in previous text mid-life is time of struggle of empty nesting, increased work demands, financial issues, frantic overload from responsibilities of two generations problems with troubled adolescents and so-called "sandwich" generation widowhood, and parental bereavement.

However, midlife may be a time of achievement and relative comfort. This can be an opportunity for couples to pursue their own interests and to spend more time together and get more life satisfaction.

As far as middle age is concerned following parameters can be taken into account to explain the life satisfaction:

- **Mental** - A close marital relationship can be viewed as a significant interpersonal resource across the adult life span, representing potentially the most intimate type of emotional support throughout the adulthood years. Conjugal support is a multidimensional construct consisting of three factors: instrumental support, emotional support and confiding (Anderson & McCulloch, 1993). Mental health of mid-adult couples is related with nature of marital relationship, differentiation of self, emotional reactivity over and above marital status. Secure relationships, loyalty and mutual emotional interest are important during this period.
- **Career challenges and job satisfaction** - Work satisfaction is at its peak in midlife years and the quality of work performance remains high although some cognitive or physical skills may decline to some extent. Patterns of work and work satisfaction do vary between men and women in middle adulthood.

  Men are more likely to improve their level of satisfaction in situations where change is possible. Women tend to withdraw or engage in complaining with co-workers. Dual career couples are required to make greater effects and adjustments which attempting to strike a balance between the simultaneous demands and pressures of their careers and family. Incase where married women held jobs outside the home they have to take care of household were along with that of outside, heading to discontent. They experience more family conflict, burn out, diffusion and role conflict.

  Twenty-first century middle-aged challenges include the globalization of work, rapid developments in information technologies, downsizing of organizations, early retirement, and concerns about pensions and health care.
- **Social satisfaction** - In the process of socialization, adults prepare for a transition in role; which involves identifying the new norms and expectations new social role as in-laws and grandparents. Adults of this age are more low abiding, traditional and resistant to change.
- **Marital satisfaction** - A recent study revealed that married and partnered middle-aged adults one more likely to view their relationships with ambivalence or indifference than their late

adulthood counterparts (Windsor & Butterworth, 2010). Security, loyalty, and mutual emotional interest become more important as especially in middle adulthood.

It is likely that middle-aged partners' identification of successful problem-solving strategies contribute to the sense that they have control over their relationship. Skilled diplomacy (an approach to solving problems that involves confrontation of the spouse about an issue, followed by a period during which the confronting spouse works to restore harmony), considered an effective skill for marital problem-solving and is practiced more often by wives than by husbands.

- **Family satisfaction** – Family is an important support group that creates joy and a sense of belonging through shared time together and expressions of love and affection. Older people with healthy marriages and positive relationships with their children enjoy their family life. This relationship worsens with conflictual and unrewarding communication.

Many adults become grandparents for the first time during middle age. They tend to define their role as grandparents, as part of their responsibility. It may be source of emotional fulfillment, feeling of companionship and satisfaction. It provides sense of proud and being valued.

Middle age also is referred as the mid-life squeeze, or the sandwich generation as family relationships in the middle age extend in both directions relationships with grown children and relationships with again parents. The family role at this stage involves maximum amounts of assistance given in both directions in the generational chain, as well as maximum responsibility for maintaining affection bonds.

Factors affecting life and marital satisfaction

The marital satisfaction or literature suggests that mid life is one of the critical periods for the relationship and life satisfaction. Similarity between partners in domains such as socioeconomic status, educational background, age, ethnicity, religion, physical attractiveness, intelligence, attitudes, and values may lead to higher levels of marital satisfaction unlikelihood of separation and divorce. However, spouses may complain of spending too much time together, particularly who have recently retired and may find themselves becoming bored with each other.

Three factors are important a marital reality; love for each other, respect for each other's life style and unconditional acceptance of each other.

Role of parents and parent-in-laws

According to the family systems theory, conflicts between husbands and wives often erupt as a result of a third party in the family. In Indian cultured context parents-in-law are frequently identified as the source of marital disputes among middle -aged couples. The support that one member of a couple gives or receives from aging parents may be perceived as interference or over involvement, can contributed to marital distress.

Giving more support to their living parent(s) than spouse may lower marital satisfaction. Others hold that the association is U-shaped with either highest depression higher ends being or highest happiness. Nonetheless, marital satisfaction does not necessarily correspond to marital stability. Some marriages are very stable despite low levels of satisfaction and much discord.

An important event in a family is the launching of a child into adult life. Parents face new adjustments as a result of the child's absence. Usually termed as the 'empty nest syndrome', which includes a decline in marital satisfaction after children leave the home. For many it may be linked to more quality time, time to pursue career interests.

Leisure in mid age

Leisure, the pleasant time after work, is an important aspect of mid aged, when they are free to pursue activities and interest of their own choice. Middle adults have more money available, more free time and paid vacations. Midlife changes may produce expanded opportunities for leisure for relaxation and time enjoyment to improve their relations and spend more time together.

Constructive and fulfilling leisure activities in middle adulthood are an important part of relaxation when adults are free to pursue activities and interests and their hobbies, sports, or reading. They also need to begin prepare psychologically for retirement.

Religion, spirituality and adult lives

During mid-age adults become more religious and consider spirituality as part of lives. Further, the influence of religion and spirituality in people's lives may change as they develop (Sapp, 2010). Some individuals who had been strongly religious in their early adult years become less so in middle age, while others became more religious in middle age (Clausen, 1993), women showing stronger interest than men.

To know more of other mid life realities the investigator reviewed available literature which have been presented in the next chapter. Review of literature

Justification of the study

As evident from the review of literature several researches, done on middle aged couples relationship in view of their adjustment and life satisfaction focused only on marital / sexual relations. Few studies conducted on adjustment pattern and life satisfaction of middle aged couples show that adjustment and life satisfaction in middle age depends on several factors. Out of these factors mental health, job conditions, social relationships, marital status and relationships with children, family environment play very significant role. Moreover most of the studies are from other countries which may not be adequately generalized to Indian families where job conditions, family constellation and relationships are significantly different.

With the advent of urbanization and modernization in India, earlier status of individuals within the family is being revised in several ways. Such changes in status might bring a lot differences in their adjustment pattern and life satisfaction. After reviewing literature investig at or unravel few facts related to middle aged generation. One is that it is the span of life where people face entirely different set of problems related to marital adjustment and life satisfaction. Till now couples had already spent a significant time with each other so that their relation is at advance and mature stage. Research reviews show that many couples in this stage view their relationship as stronger, better and more viable. On the contrary to the fewer cases where relationships weaken because of the negativity of spouse, unrealistic expectation and poor marital adjustment. Whereas other researchers report sexual compatibility as related to marital adjustment, few of them accept that other factors such as social, familial, job and other liabilities also influence their marital adjustment. Against this backdrop the present research problem has been selected for the study and stated as **"Correlates of Adjustment and Life Satisfaction among Middle Aged Married Couples".**

Following objectives have been designed for the purpose of study.

Objectives

1. To study adjustment pattern of middle aged couples.
2. To study life satisfaction among these couples.
3. To identify the correlates of adjustment and life satisfaction among middle aged couples.

Delimitations

The study was delimited to middle aged couples (50-60 years) of Narsinghpur district of Madhya Pradesh state.

Hypotheses: Null form of hypotheses have been laid down in connection with the present research as follows: There is no significant difference in adjustment pattern (health, home, social, marital, emotional and financial) of middle age males and females.

H0: There is no significant difference in adjustment (health, home, social, marital, emotional and financial) of middle aged males and females with reference to their demographic characteristics.

H0: There is no significant difference in life satisfaction (mental, job, social, marital and family) among middle aged males and females.

H0: There is no significant difference in life satisfaction (mental, job, social, marital and family) of middle aged males and females with reference to their demographic characteristics.

H0: There is no significant relationship between adjustment of middle aged husband and wife.

H0: There is no significant relationship between life satisfaction among middle aged husband and wife.

H0: There is no significant relationship between adjustment and life satisfaction of middle aged couples.

Chapter - 2

Review of Literature

The review of literature characteristically refers to available writings in books, journals and conference proceedings, unpublished proposals and thesis in context with the problem of the study. A complete evaluation of literature not only provides a vision but demonstrates how proposed study could be an addition to the field. Literature reviewed in context of the present research has been organized under the following heads:

Middle age couples adjustment

Carstensen et al. (1995) in a study on 1056 couples differing in age and marital satisfaction concluded that emotional behaviors expressed by couples differed as a function of age, gender and marital satisfaction. In older couples, the resolution of conflict was less emotionally negative and more affectionate than in middle-aged marriages. Differences between husbands / wives and between happy / unhappy marriages were also found. Wives were more affectively negative than husbands, whereas husbands were more defensive than wives, and unhappy marriages involved greater exchange of negative affect than happy marriages.

Shek (1999) examined perceived health status in 378 Chinese married couples over 2 years. Results showed that marital adjustment and marital satisfaction were concurrently related to midlife crisis symptoms, life satisfaction, and perceived health at Time 1 and Time 2. Longitudinal and prospective analyses (Time 1 predictors predicting Time 2 criterion variables) suggest that the relationships between marital quality and health measures are bidirectional in nature. Marital quality predicted changes in midlife crisis symptoms in husbands, but not in wives, marital quality predicted changes in perceived health status in wives, but not in husbands. Results also showed that mental health influenced the marital adjustment of the wives, but not the husbands, over time.

Skowron (2000) study based on couple's levels of differentiation explained substantial variance in marital adjustment: 74% of variance in husband marital adjustment scores and 61% of variance in wife marital adjustment scores were accounted for by couple differentiation of self-scores. Greater husband emotional cutoff uniquely accounted for husband and wife marital discord. Actual couples were no more similar on differentiation than were randomly matched couples. Finally, greater complementarities among couples along the specific dimensions of emotional cutoff and emotional reactivity predicted greater marital distress.

Clements & Swensen (2000) examined the relationships between several independent variables (ego development, commitment to the spouse, length of marriage, church attendance, and sex of subject) and three marital quality variables (marriage problems, expression of love, and dyadic adjustment) in a community sample of 72 married couples age 50 and up. Commitment to the spouse was the strongest and most consistent predictor of marital quality; commitment was negatively related to marriage problems and positively related to expression of love and dyadic adjustment.

Isaac & Shah (2004) analyzed 20 distressed and 20 non-distressed couples age ranged between 20-50 years from a marital and family therapy centre in the city of Bangalore, India. To find out relationship between sex roles and marital adjustment the measures included a socio demographic data sheet, the Dyadic Adjustment Scale, the Bem Sex Role Inventory and a semi-structured interview schedule for gendered experiences. The study revealed that: (a) the group as a whole showed greater femininity than masculinity; (b) more non-distressed individuals show high androgyny; (c) androgynous dyads show better marital adjustment; and (d) qualitative analysis suggests a trend for couples to move towards more gender -neutral constructions of marriage.

Bookwala (2005) in US based study on 729 respondents suggested that marital quality indices accounted for a significant amount of explained variance in physical health. Most notably, higher levels of negative spousal l behaviors uniquely contribute to physical health. These behaviors predicted more physical symptoms, chronic health problems, and physical disability, and poorer perceived health. The occurrence of negative spousal behaviors was consistently associated with poorer physical health.

Hashmi et al. (2007) explored the relationship between marital adjustment, stress and depression upon a sample of 150 (75 working /75 non-working) married women, age ranged between 18 to 50 years. Results indicated highly significant relationship between marital adjustment, depression and stress. The findings revealed that working married women have to face more problems in their married life as compared to non-working married women. The results further showed that highly educated working and non-working married women can perform well in their married life and they are free from depression as compared to less educated working and nonworking married women.

Alder (2010) conducted online survey to on 60 respondents to determine relationship between marital satisfaction and the independent variables of age, education level and courtship length. Results indicated that there was not a statistically significant relationship between marital satisfaction, age, level of education and courtship length. However, there was a negative correlation between post-engagement courtship and dyadic adjustment, indicating that, as length of engagement increases, marital adjustment decreases.

Goel & Narang (2012) studied marital adjustment, mental health and frustration reactions in males and females of middle age, from Delhi, India. The sample comprised of 150 males and 150 females (n=300) including bank employees, doctors and lecturers, within the age range of 40-55 years. Females showed high level of recreational adjustment as compared to males but males were having better group oriented attitude than females.

Lee et al. (2012) based on survey of 197 middle-aged couples indicated that couples provided more total support to and received more from their parents as a function of number of living parents, but the amount of support each parent received ('parent-adjusted support') was lower when there were more living parents but no association with the couples marital satisfaction. Husbands/ wives who gave more support to their living parent(s) reported lower marital satisfaction.

Moosavi (2012) concluded that family functioning; marital adjustment and intimacy in two groups (middle-aged and young spouses) were not significant. For subjects compared by educational status, their mean in family functioning and marital adjustment were significant, but on the intimacy scale they were the same.

Goel et al. (2013) conducted a research to study marital adjustment and mental health in 100 middle aged bank employee and doctor couples

(40-55 years) from Delhi, India. Results indicated that in bank employees, autonomy was positively correlated with family adjustment, positive self-evaluation and financial adjustment.

In middle aged doctors, autonomy was positively correlated with family adjustment and social adjustment; whereas integration of personality was found correlated with role distribution. On the other side, perception of reality was negatively correlated with recreational adjustment and role distribution. A significant interactive effect of job and age, was found on marital adjustment and mental health of middle aged couples.

Ryan et al. (2014) using a nationally representative sample of couples aged 51+ in the United States (N = 1,923 couples), investigated association of both partners' perceptions of relationship support and strain with an individual's self-rated health and functional limitations. After accounting for age, education, gender, race, and couple differences in length of marriage, results indicated that individual perceptions of support were significantly associated with higher self-rated health and fewer functional limitations. These individual-level benefits increased if the spouse also perceived positive support and low strain. Finally, the negative association of an individual's perceived support on functional limitations was greater in those with a spouse reporting low levels of perceived strain.

Middle age couples life satisfaction

Levenson et al. (1994) studied self-reported affect and autonomic and somatic physiology during three 15-min conversations (events of the day, problem area, pleasant topic) in a sample of 151 couples in long-term marriages. Couples differed in age (40-50 or 60-70) and marital satisfaction (satisfied or dissatisfied). Marital interaction in older couples was associated with more affective positivity and lower physiological arousal (even when controlling for affective differences) than in middleage couples. In terms of the relation between physiological arousal and affective experience, husbands reported feeling more negative the more they were physiologically aroused; for wives, affect and arousal were not correlated. These findings are related to theories of socio emotional change with age and of gender differences in marital behavior and health.

Jennifer et al. (1998) investigated 30 couples, with a mean age of 49, involved in a romantic relationship for an average of 20 years. Results indicated no sex differences in levels of overall intimacy, or in levels of sexual satisfaction; however the men were experiencing more sexual problems than the women. For men, sexual and emotional intimacy predicted marital satisfaction, whereas for women, recreational and emotional intimacy was the significant predictors.

Kashiwagi & Hirayama (2003) on the basis of responses from 277 pairs of middle-aged, nuclear-family couples concluded that: First, factor analysis of marital reality variables extracted three factors: love each other, respect for the husband's life style, and respect for wife's life style. Second, concerning the wife's education and income, 'respect for the wife's life style' was highest among highly educated double income couples. Third, 'love each other' was the most important predictor of marital satisfaction for both husbands and wives. Finally, 'respect for the husband's the life style' was associated with husband's satisfaction, while that for the wife's was not with wife's marital satisfaction.

Fielder & Kurpius (2005) investigated the relationship of two contextual variables (the marital relationship and stress) with the experience of menopause for 224 married midlife women. Women in dissatisfying marriages, characterized by less social support, less depth, and higher conflict, reported increased stress and more menopausal symptoms than did women in satisfying marriages. Sexual satisfaction was positively related to marital satisfaction.

Gaunt (2006) to test the hypothesis that greater similarity between partners was associated with higher levels of marital satisfaction and lower levels of negative affect, examined a sample of 248 married couples. As hypothesized, in particular, similarity on the gendered personality and values domains was more strongly associated with relationship measures, whereas similarity on the attitudes and religiosity domains showed weaker and inconsistent patterns of associations. Finally, profile-based similarity tended to be a stronger and more consistent correlate of relationship measures than difference score-based similarity.

Yeh et al. (2006) used autoregressive models, on the basis of the longitudinal data from 283 married couples, (age in 40s and 50s) who had been married for an average of 30 years. Results, for both husbands and wives, provided support for the causal sequences that proceed from sexual satisfaction to marital quality, from sexual satisfaction to marital instability and from marital quality to marital instability. Initially higher levels of sexual satisfaction resulted in an increase in marital quality, which in turn led to a decrease in marital instability over time.

Shiota & Levenson (2007) examined the relationship between similarity in big five personality factors and initial levels and 12-year trajectories of marital satisfaction in long-term couples, who were in their 40s and 60s at the beginning of the study. Across the entire sample, greater overall personality similarity predicted more negative slopes in marital satisfaction trajectories. In addition, spousal similarity on Conscientiousness and Extraversion more strongly predicted negative marital satisfaction outcomes among the midlife sample than among the older sample.

Schmitt et al. (2007) examined age and gender differences in the role of socio-economic status, personality, and marital interaction as predictors of marital satisfaction in a sample of 588 married women and men in middle and old age. Results showed a) that socio-economic factors and personality played a minor role in predicting marital satisfaction, and b) that a high quality of dyadic interaction was particularly important for the marital satisfaction of women.

Henry et al. (2007) examined age differences in positive (e.g., warm) and negative (e.g., hostile) characteristics of marital interactions between middle-aged and older couples and their association with marital satisfaction by age. Spouses' 'perception of partners' positive and negative behavior during marital interaction was assessed in general following disagreement and collaborative tasks. Older individuals reported higher marital satisfaction and perceived their spouse's behavior as less negative in general and more positive across all contexts than middle-aged individuals. Perceptions of partners' negative behavior in general and of both positive and negative behavior in the disagreement task were more closely associated with marital satisfaction for older spouses than for middle-aged spouses.

Lavalekar (2007) conducted study on 316 respondents from Maharashtra, India. The analysis indicated a significant gender difference on certain areas of emotional intelligence, namely, openness to criticism, self-management and empathy. Significant gender difference was also noted on two areas of marital satisfaction, namely, sexual relations and sharing household responsibilities, which can be traced to the socio-cultural influences.

Gorchoff et al. (2008) concluded that marital satisfaction increased in middle age, and increased marital, but not life, satisfaction was linked to the transition to an empty nest. More specifically, the transition to an empty nest increased marital satisfaction via an increase in women's enjoyment of time with their partners, but not via an increase in the quantity of that time with partners. Also, increasing marital satisfaction was not attributable to changing partners. Taken together, these findings support the utility of applying a contextualized approach focused on major life transitions to the study of long-term change in marital satisfaction.

Jan & Masood (2008) based on survey of 120 Jammu and Kashmir women, depicted that women have average level of life satisfaction at all age levels. It is found that with an increase in age, the overall life satisfaction decreases; whereas, with an increase in personal income and family income, the overall life satisfaction increases.

Seider et al. (2009) in California based study on middle-aged and older couples (N_154) engaged in a 15-minute conflict conversation, monitored physiology and emotional behavior. Verbatim transcripts of the conversations were coded into 2 lexical categories: (a) we-ness (we-words), pronouns that focus on the couple; (b) separateness (me/you-words), pronouns that focus on the individual spouses. Analyses revealed that greater we-ness was associated with a number of desirable qualities of the interaction (lower cardiovascular arousal, more positive and less negative emotional behavior), whereas greater separateness was associated with a less desirable profile (more negative emotional behavior, lower marital satisfaction). In terms of age differences, older couples used more we-ness words than did middleaged couples. Further, the associations between separateness and marital satisfaction were strongest for older wives.

Hansen et al. (2009) studied separate outcomes into cognitive (life satisfaction and self-esteem) and affective (positive and negative affect, depression, loneliness) components. Parental status has a net effect on cognitive well-being among women, as childless women report significantly lower life satisfaction and self-esteem than both mothers with residential children and empty nest mothers. However, motherhood is inconsequential for affective well-being. Among men, parental status is unrelated to any of the well-being aspects. Parental status effects are not modified by age, marital status, and education.

Huber et al. (2010) based on study of 239 couples, between the ages of 45 and 65 reported significant positive relationships between the criterion variables (rebuilding the marriage relationship and maintaining kin ties with older and younger generations) and the predictor variables (adaptive appraisal, compensating experiences, and social support), thus providing support for the position that in the face of the developmental challenges encountered relative to midlife marriage, higher levels of the primary protective factors contributing to family resilience are related to greater levels of mastery of the developmental tasks associated with midlife marital satisfaction.

Baird et al. (2011) assessed changes in life satisfaction over the lifespan through cross-sectional and longitudinal features to isolate age-related changes from confounding factors including instrumentation effects and cohort effects. Although estimated satisfaction trajectories varied somewhat across studies, two consistent findings emerged. First, both studies show that life satisfaction does not decline over much of adulthood. Second, there is a steep decline in life satisfaction among those older than 70. The British data also showed a relatively large increase in satisfaction from the 40s to the early 70s. Thus, age differences in well-being can be quite large and deserve increased empirical and theoretical attention.

Kouros & Cummings (2011) collected information from 296 America based couples on marital satisfaction, marital conflict and depressive symptoms annually reported for three years. Results suggested that for husbands, transactional relations between marital satisfaction and depressive symptoms identified: high levels of depressive symptoms predicted subsequent decreases in marital satisfaction and decreased marital satisfaction predicted subsequent elevations in depressive symptoms over time. For wives, high levels of marital conflict predicted subsequent elevations in depressive symptoms over time. Cross-partner results indicated that husbands‘ depressive symptoms were also related to subsequent declines in wives‘ marital satisfaction.

Kasimatis & Guastello (2012) based on responses of 432 mothers, of college going students, on the Parental Authority Questionnaire and the Satisfaction with Life Scale, concluded that work role was found to be non-significant in relation to midlife mothers‘ life satisfaction, whereas an authoritative parenting style was significantly correlated to this same variable. Employed mothers did report being more stressed, especially when their children were younger, but again maternal work role was not predictive of these women’s life satisfaction in midlife.

Pinto & Neto (2012) based on 193 participants with a mean age of 51.64, found no gender differences regarding the satisfaction with sex life. Characteristics indicative of the quality of a relationship (Eros, commitment, sexual desire, and romantic loneliness) were related to the level of sexual satisfaction. Measures of well being (satisfaction, life satisfaction, and self-esteem) were also related to sex life satisfaction.

Hasani et al. (2012) conducted study for evaluation of the relationships and links between the factors of emotional intelligence and marital satisfaction in 122 Academic members of Rafsanjan University of Medical Sciences. Overall, emotional intelligence and marital satisfaction were not linked to the variables of gender and age. Of many aspects of marital satisfaction, interpersonal and empathy aspects were meaningfully related to the variable of gender. Also, of many aspects of emotional intelligence, the one for responsibility between men and women was only meaningfully different. Generally, all the variables of emotional intelligence and marital satisfaction had a statistical meaningful relationship. 37% of marital satisfaction is predictable by emotional intelligence.

Zainah et al. (2012) based on demographic variables among 423 married couples aimed to ascertain the differences in marital satisfaction (measured by enriched marital satisfaction scale). Results indicated significant differences in marital satisfaction based on the length of marriage and income.

Kim (2013) aimed to identify the relationship among marital intimacy, sex communication, sexual satisfaction, and the marital satisfaction, and reveal factors of the middle-aged women's marital satisfaction. The subjects were chosen by convenience sampling of middle-aged women in Korea. Marital intimacy, sexual satisfaction, and marital satisfaction averaged 3.52, 3.19, and 2.66 (out of 4) respectively, and the average score for sexual communication was 3.09 (out of 5). Marital satisfaction had a positive correlation with marital intimacy, sex communication, and sexual satisfaction. Marital intimacy, sexual satisfaction, and job status were the influencing factors on marital satisfaction.

Atta et al. (2013) examined the role of trust in marital satisfaction in a sample of 140 couples including 70 single & 70 dual-career couples. Enrich Marital Satisfaction Scale (Fowers & Olson, 1993), and Trust Scale (Rempel, Holmes & Zanna, 1985) was used to measure the constructs. Multiple regression analysis demonstrated trust as significant predictor of marital satisfaction. Significant gender differences were found in trust for both single and dual-career couples.

Pethtel & Chen (2014) concluded that dispositional variables, including personality factors, emotion regulation strategies, and affect, accounted for a significant amount of variance in predicting life satisfaction. However, life regrets uniquely accounted for variance in life satisfaction more so than dispositional factors.

Dabone & Tawiah (2014) carried out study in order to find marital satisfaction level of 320 married people, Young married people (18 – 40 years) and old married people (41 – 60 year and above), in the Sunyani Municipality of the Brong-Ahafo Region. The results of the findings revealed that younger married people were significantly more dissatisfied than the older ones.

Molina et al. (2015) studied sexual life satisfaction of 142 couples, age range 40-60 years, of family health centers and differences between the perception of satisfaction and the sex life of each partner. 66% of women and 84% of men reported being very or somewhat satisfied with their sex lives. Slight concordance was found between the responses of the partners in relation to satisfaction with their sexual life. Moreover, a slight degree of agreement was found between the sexual life satisfaction reported by women and their partners' perceptions of the women's sexual life satisfaction. Additionally, a slight degree of agreement was reported between the sexual life satisfaction reported by men and their partners' perceptions of the men's sexual life satisfaction.

D'Zurillaet al. (1998) suggested that social problem-solving ability increases from young adulthood (ages 17–20) to middle-age (ages 40–55) and then decreases in older age (ages 60–80). Specifically, compared to younger adults, middle-aged individuals scored higher on positive problem orientation and rational problem solving, and lower on negative problem orientation, impulsivity/carelessness style, and avoidance style. Compared to older adults, middle-aged individuals scored higher on positive problem orientation and rational problem solving. Across age groups, gender differences were found on positive problem orientation and negative problem orientation. Within the young adult group, gender differences were also found on impulsivity/carelessness style.

Singh & Singh (2005) indicated that women's psychosocial health status may likely to get affected during middle age due to psychological changes occurring in this phase primarily because of biological changes and changes in the familial environment. Programmed interventions like, meditation, relaxation and other sensitization programs, aiming at lifestyle changes will change their attitudes, behaviors, cognitions, quality of life, thereby maintaining their overall status.

White & Myers (2006) examined the relationship among chronological age, subjective age, wellness, and life satisfaction among women (N = 224) between 35 and 65 years old. Women whose subjective age was less than or equal to their chronological age reported greater wellness; total wellness was a significant predictor of life satisfaction.

Ko et al. (2007) identified coupled profiles of successful aging in middle-aged (n = 139; wives, M = 43.8 years old; husbands, M = 45.6 years old) and older adult married couples (n = 148; wives, M = 62.0 years old; husbands, M = 64.4 years old). Results indicated that a large group of couples scored favorably across domains of successful aging. Unevenness across domains was ide ntified, in that some groups involved a disassociation between marital satisfaction and health outcomes.

Smith et al. (2009) based on 300 middle-aged and older married couples responses, reported less negative affect during disagreement and rated spouses as warmer than did middle-aged couples. However, these effects were eliminated when older couples' greater marital satisfaction was controlled. For observed behavior, older couples displayed little evidence of greater positivity and reduced negativity—especially women. During collaboration, older couples displayed a unique blend of warmth and control, suggesting a greater focus on emotional and social concerns during problem solving.

Rahmani et al. (2009) used 292 married men, and women aged 19-58 years from selected hospitals in Tehran while visiting their hospitalized relatives. Marital satisfaction significantly relates to sexual satisfaction (P= 0/00). There was also a significant relation between sexual satisfaction and the following variables: age difference of couples (P= 0.04), length of marital life (P= 0.05), and a drug abused participant (P= 0.007). Of these variables, only the age difference of couples significantly relates to marital satisfaction (0.00).

Windsor & Butterworth (2010) examined age group differences in selfreported supportive, aversive, ambivalent, and indifferent partner relations, in a large sample of midlife (aged 40-44 at baseline, n = 1,719) and older (aged 60-64 at baseline, n = 1,675) married and partnered adults assessed on two occasions 4 years apart. Older adults, particularly older men, were more likely to rate their relationship as supportive and less likely to rate their relationship as aversive relative to midlife adults. Midlife adults were more likely to provide ambivalent or indifferent assessments (as opposed to supportive assessments) of their relationship relative to older adults.

Yuan et al. (2010) in a California study based on 149 middle-aged and older married couples engaged in a 15-min discussion of an area of marital conflict, measured autonomic and somatic physiological activity during the conversation, and emotional behaviors were recorded and subsequently coded.

Study found that during 20-s periods of down-regulation (where physiology transitioned from high arousal to low arousal), couples showed an increase in positive emotional behavior compared with periods without down-regulation. The finding was quite robust, suggesting that the undoing effect of positive emotion generalizes across age, sex, and marital satisfaction.

Seider & Herschel (2011) examined the relationships between discrete emotion sequences and marital satisfaction in middle-aged (N = 82) and older (N = 74) couples, in California in and whether this relationship is moderated by age and gender. The study focused on discrete emotion sequences initiated by three antecedent emotions (anger, contempt and sadness) previously associated with distressed marriages. Results revealed significant associations between discrete emotion sequences and marital satisfaction for 11 of the 39 discrete emotion sequences examined. The findings indicated that the relationships between discrete emotion sequences and marital satisfaction did not consistently differ as a function of age, but when they did, they tended to be stronger for older couples.

Berg et al. (2011) this study based on 300 middle-aged and older couples who completed measures of perceptions of collaboration, cognitive ability, marital satisfaction, an errand task and judged their spouse's affiliation. Older adults (especially men) endorsed cognitive compensation and interpersonal enjoyment and reported using collaboration more frequently than middle-aged adults. Greater need for cognitive compensation was related to lower cognitive ability only for older wives. Greater marital satisfaction was associated with greater interpersonal enjoyment. These two functions related to reports of more frequent use of collaboration and perceptions of spousal affiliation in a collaborative task.

Fiori & Denckla (2012) examined the association between various aspects of social support and depressive symptoms in a sample of 6,767 middle-aged adults from one wave of the Wisconsin (longitudinal study separately among men and women). Results found that the receipt of emotional support was associated with mental health in women only, whereas the provision of emotional and instrumental support was associated with mental health among men and women, but with varying patterns.

Ayalon et al. (2013) surveyed 2723 couples over the age of 50, residing in the US to find out associations between loneliness and subjective appraisals of marital relationship as well as reciprocal associations of loneliness in married men and women. The model suggested that subjective appraisals of the relationship with spouse play a major role in one's sense of loneliness. In addition, loneliness in men and women shares reciprocal associations. The model explained 24% and 29% of the variability in loneliness reported by married men and women, respectively. Results indicated that capitalizing and enhancing one's social life might also be beneficial for his or her partner.

Momtaz et al. (2013) studied 300 couples aged 50 years and older. Interdependence analyses revealed significant association between older adults‘ attitudes toward aging and the attitudes of their spouses (intra class correlation =0.59; P,0.001), and similar interdependence was found for psychological wellbeing (intraclass correlation =0.57; P,0.001). The findings from AMOS revealed that the proposed model fits the data (CMIN/degrees of freedom =3.23; goodness-of-fit index =0.90; confirmatory fit index =0.91; root mean square error of approximation =0.08). Results of the actor–partner independence model indicated that older adults 'psychological well-being is significantly predicted by their spouses' attitudes toward aging, both among older men (critical ratio =2.92; P,0.01) and women (critical ratio =2.70; P,0.01). Husbands' and wives' own reports of their attitudes toward aging were significantly correlated with their own and their spouses' psychological well-being.

Chapter - 3

Research Methodology

Methodology is the logic of scientific investigation and techniques. Which includes description, explanation and justification of methods and not the method themselves. It contains the standards and principles employed to guide the choice of structure process and use of methods, as directed by the underlying paradigm.

The purpose of this chapter is to describe various aspects of conducting a research scientifically. The steps adopted by the researcher, study design, methods and techniques used have been appropriately described along with logic behind them to attain the objectives of the study.

This chapter is divided into following subheads:

- Research design
- Locale of the study
- Sample and sampling procedure
- Procedure of collection of data
- Tools used for data collection
- Statistics used for analysis and interpretation of data

Research design

This research is descriptive in nature. Descriptive research includes surveys and fact finding enquiries of different kinds. Survey method was adopted for the purpose of data collection, which is commonly used in Human Development to collect self-report data from study participants. The survey method is fact finding with adequate interpretation in the light of the norms and essentially a method of quantitative description of the general characteristics of a group.

Locale of the study

The study was conducted in Narsinghpur district of Madhya Pradesh state in central India, selected for various reasons- first there was no prior systematic effort to study middle age form human development point of view, secondly the availability of various groups of respondents. Most importantly due to the long process of approaching the respondents and collecting information it was required to make several visits to the participants. Therefore being the home town of the investigator this area was selected so as to facilitate the whole process of research.

Sample and sampling procedure

555 Middle aged couples (making total N= 1110) between 50-60 years of age were purposively selected for the study. Parents of secondary to college students, between the desired age group, were contacted (personal in-home surveys) to seek permission and decide for convenient time of data collection. Couples from banks, post office, different shopping premises, parks and other public places (personal street intercept survey), between 50-60 years of age and willing to participate were also taken as respondents for study. Before starting survey work, investigator took their written permission along with their basic information like name, age, address, suitable time to approach for conducting survey.

Procedure of collection of data

The investigator explained the purpose of the study and collected the required information by contacting each couple personally by using survey technique.Data were collected in very informal manner by the investigator after establishing good rapport with the couples. The survey questions were formulated in Hindi, which helped in creating better understanding, intimate relationship, confidence and trust of respondents towards the investigator. Probing was done wherever it was needed.

Tools used for data collection

Standardized tools were used to collect information on adjustment and life satisfaction of middle age couples. These were the tests suitable for the selected age group with well-established reliability and validity. Investigator also developed two survey instruments to elicit personal information of respondents and to find out their perception about various factors of adjustment and life satisfaction. Following table presents summary of the tools used to collect data on various aspects of the study

Table 3.1: Tools used for data collection

S.No.	*Variables*	*Tool*	*Remark*
1.	Socio-demographic profile of respondents	General Information Blank	Prepared by the investigator in the year (2014)
2.	Adjustment	Old Age Adjustment Inventory to measure adjustment in six areas – health,home, social, marital, emotional and financial	Developed by Shamshad Hussain and Jashbir Kaur (1995)
3.	Life satisfaction	Life Satisfaction Scale measuring life satisfaction in five areas – mental, job, social, marital and family	Developed by Pramod Kumar and Jayshree Dhyani in the year (1988)
4.	Perception of middle aged couple about the various factors affecting life satisfaction and marital adjustment	Factors of Adjustment and Satisfaction in Middle Adulthood included- areas; physical illness and chronic disease, mental health, positive thinking and decision making, family environment	Prepared by the investigator in the year 2014)

Description of tools

General Background Information Blank: General Background Information Blank was prepared to elicit information on couples' gender, age, education, occupation, monthly-income, residence area, family type, religion, years married, age at the time of marriage, religion of spouse (if different), type of marriage. Information related to children like gender, age, educational status, marital status, occupation, monthly income, resident place (if not staying with the couple), reason for staying separate (like education, job, maladjustment, quarrel and other family members (sharing household) like relationship with the respondent, age, gender, education status, marital status, occupation and responsibility of other family member, not staying in the same household was also included. **(Annexure-I)**

Old Age Adjustment Inventory (by Shamshad Hussain and Jashbir Kaur): There are 125 items in all measuring the adjustment of old aged people into six area shealth, home, social, marital, emotional and financial.

Scoring: One score is to be given to the response in the direction of adjustment (Yes response) 0 (Zero) to the response in the direction of maladjustment (No response). Undecided category is not to be given any score. The responses given by the test takers can also be scored with the help of scoring key. The keyed response is to be assigned one score. Score stencils of each of the six areas are available for convenient scoring on the answer sheet. Hence, the higher score indicates better adjustment. The responses are scored area wise. The sum of scores in different areas provides measure of overall adjustment. **(Annexure-II).**

Life Satisfaction Scale (by Pramod Kumar and Jayshree Dhyani): The Life Satisfaction Scale (LSS) in its final form consists of 54 highly discriminating items-45 positively worded and 9 negatively worded. These items are presented in a 3-point rating format.

Scoring: A numerical value of 3, 2 and 1 is assigned to the 'True', 'Partially true' and 'Not true' response categories for all the items, except for negativelyworded items, i.e. 1, 3, 4, 6, 7, 14, 26, 27 & 34, in which ease reverse scoring is applicable. The sum of these values gives the overall life satisfaction score for the subject. Since, the responses contributing to life satisfaction are given a score, the higher the total score, the higher would be the life satisfaction. The scale can also be scored area-wise if need be **(Annexure-III).**

Factors of Adjustment and Satisfaction in Middle Adulthood Check list: In mid-age due to aging effect health start degrading, this not only affect their physical capabilities and economical productivity, but also cause significant psychological implications, like feeling of incapability, increased dependencies, depression. Expenses on medicines and chronic diseases increase financial burden which may cause sad and tense family environment, poor mental health and shattered peace. In this age due to overloaded burden from taking care of children and parent, adjusting family budget to fulfill needs of family members, they lack time for family, have little time to social life participation and getting along with others which may affect their social life satisfaction. Busy in making adjustments between family, social and professional responsibilities, mid-age couples tend to think too much which may cause feeling of low-satisfaction and unhappiness, peevish behavior, irritation and loose temperament, lack of focus or concentration, sad and feeling isolated. Being executive head of the family mid-age couples have to take decision on almost all family matters ranging from mundane household decisions to selecting colleges and making investments for better future. This requires a lot of energy and demands great responsibility.

Till mid-age, couples have faced numerous good and bad instances of married life together also develop a very good understanding of each other's behavior and attitude. Spouse becomes the best companion. However, there are many behavioral pattern of spouse which one does not like and accept. These patterns cause tensed family environment. Family becomes the binding force in relation between mid -aged couples. Family gives sense of togetherness and fulfillment in life but in many cases family become the major source of pain and unhappiness due to lack of cooperation and respect, stubborn nature of family members, children being in bad friendship, indifferent nature of family members.

Procedure for development of check list: Pilot survey was conducted on middle aged couples to find out their perception on family factors of adjustment and life satisfaction. Researcher interviewed 50 middle age men and women (not included in final sample), between 50 to 60 years, to point out factors that contribute to their healthy adjustment from different groups and from different places. They were asked to give descriptive answers. To know the perception of middle aged people about various correlates of life satisfaction and marital adjustment, a questionnaire was developed in house. Although many environmental influences may decide adjustment pattern and life satisfaction of individuals but investigator concentrated on family factors of influence to pin point study and elicit in depth information of these factors.

Based on what these people reported about problems and conflict in their life the researcher drew up a check list. This check list was further given to 2 psychologists, 2 sociologists and 5 Human Development professors in order to ensure the validity of the questionnaire. Finally investigator incorporated the suggestions of experts and finalized the questionnaire. Final form of inventory contains 81 statements categorized in five areas. Area wise number of items is given below-

1. Physical illness and chronic disease – 14 items
2. Mental health – 16 items
3. Positive thinking and decision making – 16 items
4. Relation with life partner – 20 items
5. Family environment – 15 items

   (See Annexure-IV for details)

Scoring: Respondent has to tick mark (√) statements which in their opinion lower their adjustment and life satisfactions. They are free to mark as many options as they find appropriate in their opinion.

Area wise raw scores can also be obtained by adding all the Yes responses in each area category and can be used for further comparison of groups and statistical analysis with minimum score 0 for each area and maximum possible score as the number of items in that category.

Statistics used for analysis and interpretation of data

The data were consolidated, tabulated and analyzed in term of quantitative or qualitative interpretation of fact using following statistical tools.

Frequency distributions to organize and present number counts so that the information can be interpreted more easily - Frequency distribution data have been shown in table or graph and pie charts.

Percentage (%) ratio to convert data in dimensionless number (pure number) - Percentage value is computed by multiplying the numeric value of the ratio by 100.

Mean to measure central tendency- The mean is equal to the sum of all the values in the data set divided by the number of values in the data set. So, if we have $x_{1,}$ $x_{2,}$ ...,$x_{n,}$ values in a data set and they have values $\bar{x}$ (pronounced x bar), is:

$$\bar{x} = \frac{(x_1 + x_2 + ... + x_n)}{n}$$

Standard deviation (SD, σ or *s*) to quantify the amount of variation or dispersion of a set of data values - A standard deviation close to 0 indicates that the data points tend to be very close to the mean (also called the expected value) of the set, while a high standard deviation indicates that the data points are spread out over a wider range of values.

$$\sigma = \sqrt{\frac{\Sigma(x - \bar{x})2}{N}}$$

where

σ = the standard deviation

x = each value in the population

$\bar{x}$ = the mean of the values

N = the number of values (the population)

Student 't' to find out significance of difference between means- Statistical significance indicates whether or not the difference between two 'groups' averages most likely reflects a "real" difference in the population from which the groups were samples.

Formula-

$$t = \frac{M1 - M2}{\sigma D} \frac{\text{Difference between means}}{\text{Standard error of difference between means}}$$

$$\text{Where SED or } \sigma D = \sqrt{\frac{\sigma 1^2}{N1} + \frac{\sigma 2^2}{N2}}$$

Karl Pearson's Correlation Coefficient for the measurement of linear relationship between two variables- If X and Y are two variables formula calculating for correlation used is

$$r = \frac{\Sigma XY - (\Sigma X)(\Sigma Y)}{\sqrt{\left[\Sigma X^2 - \frac{(\Sigma X)2}{N}\right]\left[\Sigma Y^2 - \frac{(\Sigma Y)2}{N}\right]}}$$

Where,

r = correlation cofficient

ΣX = Sum of X series variable

ΣY = Sum of Y series variable

ΣXY = Sum of product of ΣXY

ΣX^2= Sum of square of X variable

ΣY^2= Sum of square of Y variable

All the analysis was done with the help of SPSS 16.0 version system and tested at 5% level of significance.

Graphical and diagrammatical presentations of data have also been included wherever required.

Chapter - 4

Result and Discussion

This chapter furnishes the findings and results deduced from analysis of data obtained by different groups of middle aged people. The data have been organized and analyzed on the basis of objectives set forth for the present research. The chapter highlights the findings under following subheads:

Part I: Demographic profile of respondents

Part II: Adjustment of middle aged males and females

Part III: Demographic factors of adjustment among middle aged males and females

Part IV: Life satisfaction of middle aged males and females

Part V: Demographic factors of life satisfaction in middle aged males and females

Part VI: Association between adjustment of husband and wife and life satisfaction of husband and wife

Part VII: Association between adjustment and life satisfaction of middle aged couples

Part VIII: Factors of adjustment and satisfaction in middle adulthood

Part I: Demographic Profile Of Respondents

Prior to in depth assessment of the different aspects included under the study, it is important to know general background of the sampled respondents. An understanding of characteristics of the respondents is highly relevant to the study since these components play important role in adjustment and satisfaction of an individual. This section deals with general information, categorized as personal profile and family profile of the respondents, which helped to classify respondents for further analysis, (Appendix-I). Presented in the tables below, presented in terms of frequency as well as percentages (in parenthesis)-

Table 1: Demographic characteristics of middle aged couples

S. No.	*Variables*	*Frequency and Percentage (%)*			
1.	Age				
	Husband / Wife	50-55	55-60		Total Females
	50-55	150 (27.04)	319 (57.47)		469 (84.51)
	55-60	0	86 (15.49)		86 (15.49)
	Total Males	150 (27.04)	405 (72.96)		
2.	Education				
	Husband / Wife	Illiterate - Primary	Metric - higher secondary	Graduation and above	Total Females
	Illiterate–primary	145 (26.13)	84 (15.13)	31 (5.58)	260 (46.84)
	Metric - higher secondary	12 (2.16)	79 (14.23)	85 (15.33)	176 (31.72)
	Graduation and above	3 (0.54)	14 (2.53)	102 (18.37)	119 (21.44)
	Total Males	160 (28.83)	177 (31.89)	218 (39.28)	
3.	Occupation				
	Husband / Wife	Jobs/Service	Business	Retired	Total Females
	Jobs / Service	27 (4.86)	6 (1.08)	1(0.18)	34 (6.12)
	Business	2 (0.36)	6 (1.08)	0	8 (1.44)
	Retired	0	0	1(0.18)	1 (0.18)
	Home maker	307 (55.32)	185 (33.33)	20 (3.61)	512 (92.26)
	Total Males	336 (60.54)	197 (35.49)	22 (3.97)	
4.	Age at the time of marriage				
	Husband / Wife	Below 18-21	21-30	Above30	Total Females
	Below 18-21	127 (22.88)	230 (41.44)	4 (0.73)	361 (65.05)
	21-30	0	179 (32.25)	8 (1.44)	187 (33.69)
	Above 30	0	0	7 (1.26)	7 (1.26)
	Total Males	127 (22.88)	409 (73.69)	19 (3.43)	

- **Age:** Majority of the females belong to 50-55 years age group (84.5% of total female respondents). On the contrary most of the males are in 55-60 years age range (73%) of total male respondents. It evinces that in general there is gap in age of husband and wife. In majority of cases males are older than their female counterparts (57.47%). There is no couple where wife is older than husband.
- **Education:** Percentage of females in the illiterate to primary category is more (46.84% as against 28.8% males). Percentage of males is more in graduation and above category (39.3% as against 21.4% females), whereas matriculation to high secondary percentage of male and females is more or less same. This shows

that males are more educated than females. In general 26.13% couples are educated up to primary level and in 18.37 cases both (husband and wife) are educated at least up to graduate level.

- **Occupation:** In general 60.72% of males whereas only 5.76% females are in various jobs / service. More than one third of the males (35.13%) are running their own business (as against only 1.44% females). More than ninety per cent women are home makers and not in any paid jobs. Only 4.86 couples (both husband and wife) are in service and 1.08% in business.
- **Age at the time of marriage:** Majority of males reported their age of marriage between 21 to 30 years and females below 21 years. It reflects that more women got married at early age than males. It is also evident from the age gap between couples.

Demographic profile of respondents at a glance

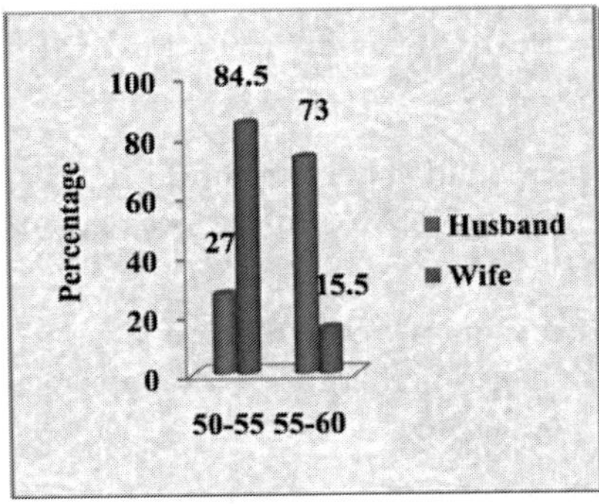

Figure 4.1. Age of middle age couples

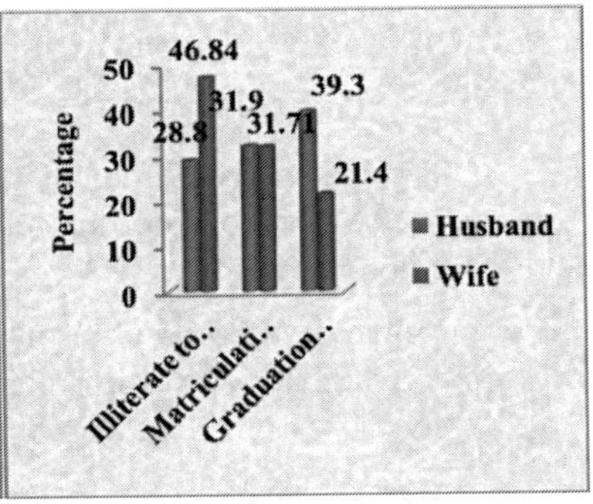

Figure 4.2. Education of middle age couples

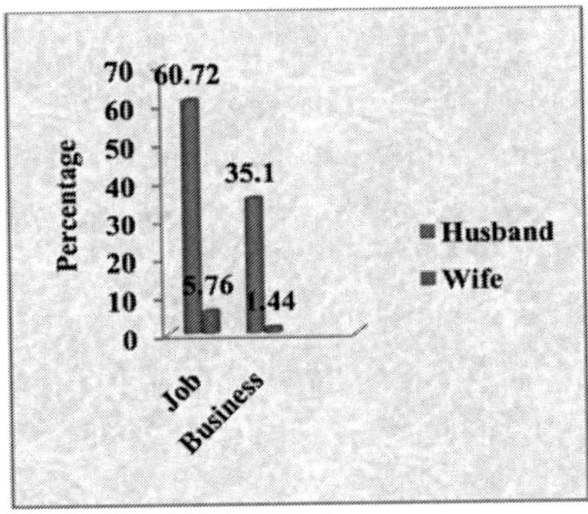

Figure 4.3. Occupation of middle age couples

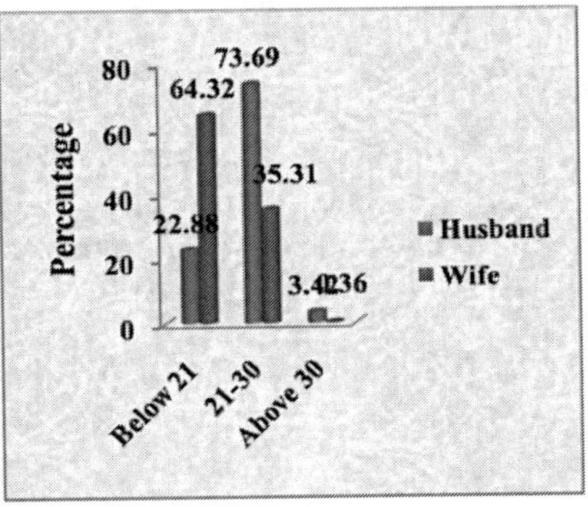

Figure 4.4. Age at the time of marriage of middle age couples

Table 2: Family information of respondents

S. No.	*Family information*	*Categories*	*Frequency and Percentage (%)*
1.	Type of family	Nuclear	342 (61.63)
2.	Religion	Joint	213 (38.37)
		Hindu	490 (88.28)
3.	Married years	Muslim	27 (4.86)
		Sindhi	13 (2.34)
		Panjabi	4 (0.74)
		Jain	21 (3.78)
		20-30	124 (22.35)
		30-40	431 (77.65)
4.	Monthly family income	Below15000	241 (43.42)
		15000-30000	216 (38.91)
		30000-45000	97 (17.41)
		Above45000	43 (7.74)

- Type of family: Although nuclear family system is more prevalent (61.63%) but more than one third (38.37%) of the respondents belong to joint family.
- Religion: Majority of respondents follow Hindu religion (88.28%) and 4.86% are Muslims. Percentage of other religion followers is very low as evident from the above table.
- Married years: 77.65% couples are married for more than 30 years whereas 22.35% couples are married for less than 30 years but more than 20 years.
- Monthly family income: In majority of cases (43.42%) family income is below Rs. 15000 per month followed by 15000 to 45000 (38.9%). Income between Rs. 30000-45000 income category has been reported by 17.4% whereas about only eight percent respondents reported their family income above 45000.

Family profile of respondents at a glance

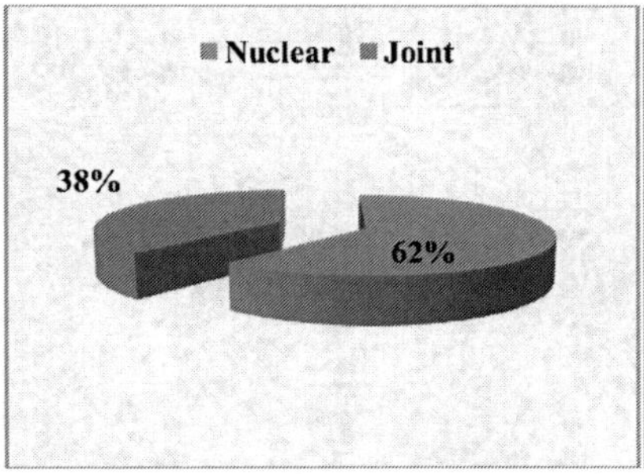

Figure 4.5. Type of family of middle age couples

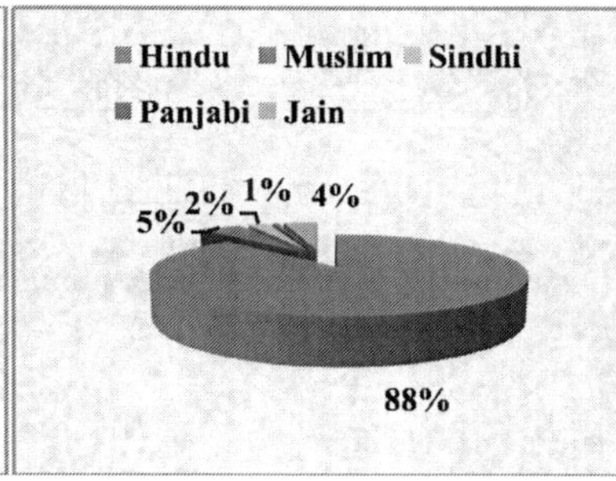

Figure 4.6. Religion of middle age couples

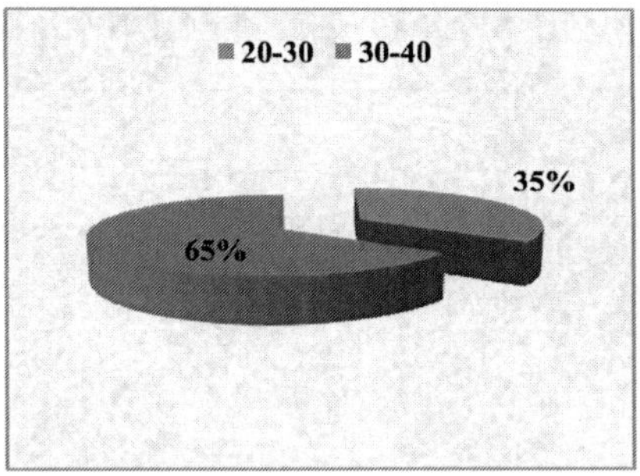

Figure 4.7. Married years of middle age Couples

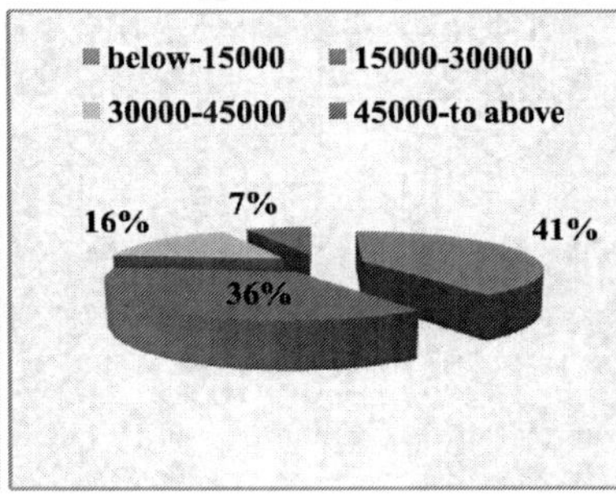

Figure 4.8. Monthly family income of middle age couples

Information on Children of Middle Aged Couples

As mentioned earlier middle age couples of the families were included the study.

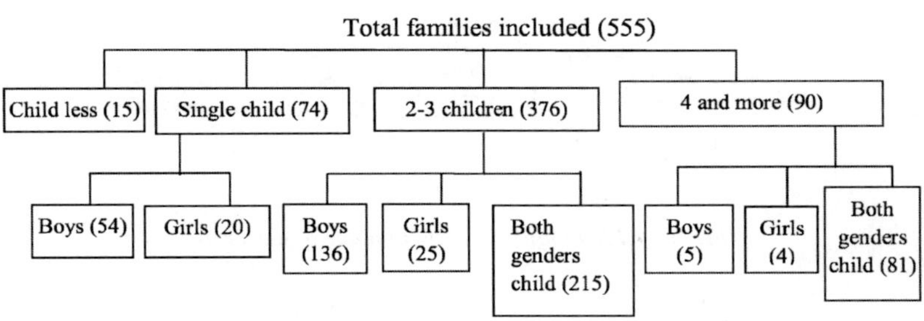

Figure 4.9. Family wise number of sex of children

Age of children

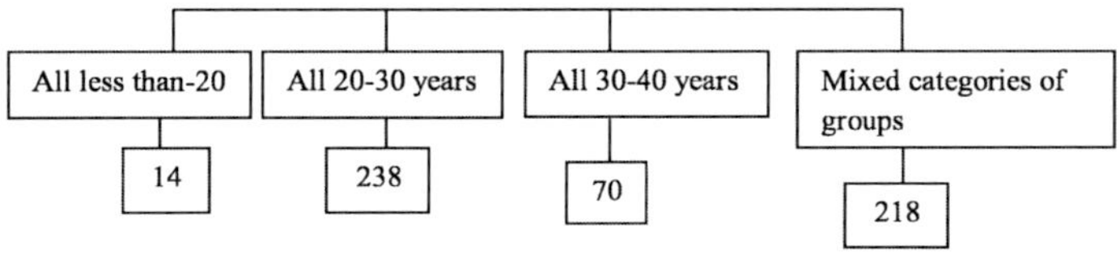

Figure 4.10. Family wise age of children

Education of children

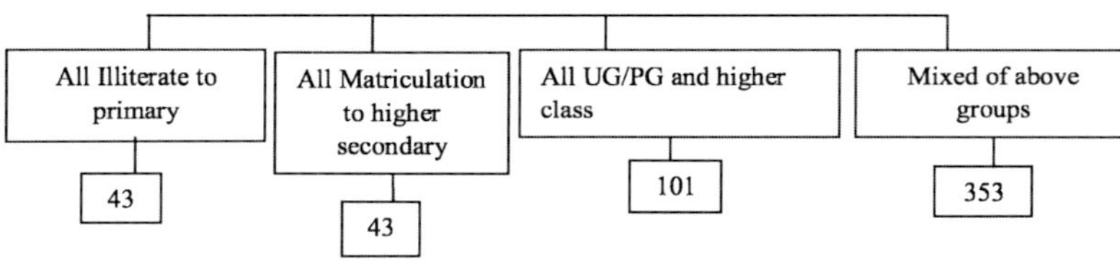

Figure 4.11. Family wise education of children

Married status of children

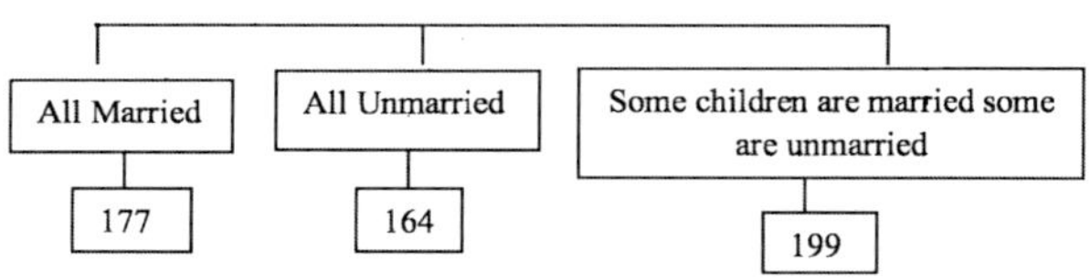

Figure 4.12. Family wise married status of children

Living place of children

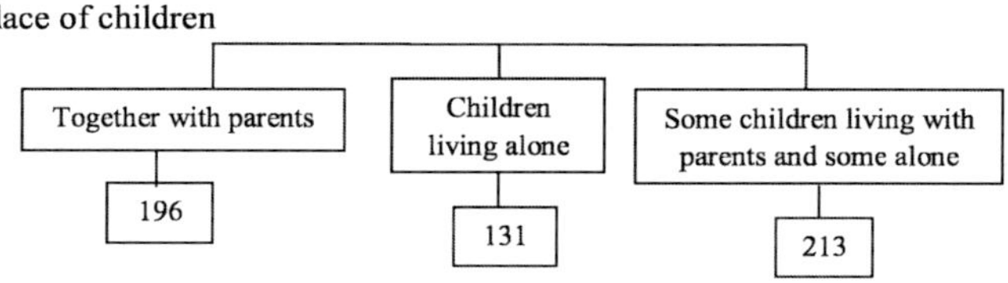

Figure 4.13. Family wise living place of children

From the above table following points can be deduced

1. Families with male child only are comparatively much higher than the families with female child only. This pattern indicates towards a major social evil - to give more importance to male child than female child. Families wish to have at least one male child and which is the reason that number of families with female child/children only is very less compared to families with male child only.
2. In majority of families, all children are in the age group 20-30 years followed by 30-40 years age group (70 families) and in 218 families children are in different age groups. In fourteen families children are below 20 years of age.
3. In 101 families all children are educated at least under graduation and above and 43 up to matriculation / higher secondary. In 353 families they are of different education level whereas in 43 families children are either illiterate / primary level only.
4. In 177 families all children are married and 164 families all children are unmarried. In 199 families some children are married and some are unmarried.

   Whereas 186 families married male children living with parent home. It was found that in most of the families, married son lives with parents.
5. In 196 families all children live together with middle age couples and 131 families all children living away for their education and job from middle age couples. Whereas 213 families some children living together with parents and some living away from middle age couples.

Part II: Adjustment of Middle aged Males and Females

As mentioned in earlier chapter adjustment of middle aged couples was assessed by 'Old Age Adjustment Inventory', measuring adjustment in six areas; health, home, social, marital, emotional and financial. Raw scores for adjustment are given in appendix-VI. Calculated Means (shows an average) of husband and wife for adjustment scores, SD values (shows the amount of variation or dispersion of a set of data values) and t ratio (shows significance of difference between means of husband and wife adjustment results) have been presented in the following table-

H0: There is no significant difference in adjustment (health, home, social, marital, emotional and financial) of middle aged males and females.

Table 3: M±SD and t-values for adjustment of middle aged males and females

S. No.	*Areas of Adjustment*	*Male Mean± SD*	*Female Mean± SD*	*T-values*
1.	Health	19.91±3.763	19.51±4.553	1.581
2.	Home	21.33±3.387	21.10±3.782	1.079
3.	Social	16.31±2.825	16.15±3.207	.904
4.	Marital	13.89±2.235	13.67±2.379	1.586
5.	Emotional	15.96±3.237	15.55±3.669	1.978*
6.	Financial	9.86±1.852	9.53±2.093	2.810*

* Significant

As evident from the above table, out of the six adjustment areas, t values for only two adjustment areas; emotional and financial are significant, indicating significant difference in emotional and financial adjustment of middle aged males and females. Comparisons of means evinces that emotional and financial adjustment of males is better than females, It may be due to the fact that in typical Indian families males have more authority in making decisions, especially in financial matters. In others areas of adjustment; health, home, social and marital t values calculated are not significant and helps to conclude that in areas of adjustment; health, home, social and marital, adjustment of middle aged males and females is more or less similar. This study is also in congruence with other research evincing that emotional behavior expressed by couples differed as a function of gender (Carstensen et al., 1995). Mid age couples become more realistic and practical about their relation and family issues.

Part III: Demographic Factors of Adjustment Among Middle Aged Males and Females

To find out demographic differences in adjustment of middle aged males and females with reference to demographic variables under study (including age, education, occupation, age at the time of marriage, type of family and married years), Mean± SD and t values were calculated for each area of adjustment. These have been presented in the tables below -

Demographic factors of health adjustment

H0: There is no significant difference in health adjustment of middle aged males and females with reference to their demographic characteristics.

Table 4: M±SD and t-values for health adjustment of middle aged with reference of demographic variables

S. No.	*Demographic Variables*	*Categories Mean± SD*	*Male Mean± SD*	*Female*	*T-values*
1.	**Age**	50-55 (a)	19.70±3.94	19.46±4.63	.559
		55-60 (b)	19.99±3.69	19.77±4.06	.488
		t-values (a) (b)	.793	.566	
2.	**Education**	Illiterate to primary (a)	20.55±3.47	20.05±4.29	1.24
		Matriculation to higher secondary (b)	19.36±3.86	18.60±4.67	1.66
		Graduation and above (c)	19.89±3.82	19.69±4.74	.412
		t-values (a) (b)	2.97*	3.34*	
		t-values (b) (c)	1.36	1.95	
		t-values (a) (c)	1.73 .	734	
3.	**Occupation**	Jobs / Service (a) Business (b)	20.07±3.67 19.76±3.88	20.16±4.46 15.38±5.87	.122 3.06*
		t-values (a) (b)	.909	2.54*	
4.	**Age at the time of marriage**	Below18-21 (a)	19.72±3.97	19.49±4.56	.502
		21-30 (b)	19.95±3.73	19.57±4.55	1.09
		Above 30 (c)	20.32±3.07	18.50±3.53	.788
		t-values (a) (b) .	629	.195	
		t-values (b) (c) .	422	.330	
		t-values (a) (c)	.629	.305	
5.	**Type of family**	Nuclear (a)	19.71±3.88	19.32±4.65	1.19
		Joint (b)	20.22±3.54	19.82±4.37	1.04
		t-values (a) (b)	1.54	1.24	
6.	**Married years**	20-30 (a)	20.07±3.66	27.42±2.74	22.34*
		30-40 (b)	19.82±3.81	19.50±4.49	1.04
		t-values (a) (b)	.728	22.39*	

Analysis and Interpretation: when compared for health adjustments of middle age with different demographical factors above table indicated following facts:

There is no significant difference in health adjustment of middle aged males and females of different age groups. It may be concluded that health adjustment is not affected by age of middle aged couples.

- Although there is no significant difference in health adjustment of males and females of various education levels but somehow it is strange to note that in both the groups (male as well as female) less educated (illiterate to primary) group mean is significantly higher than other two levels of education. Less educated middle aged people show better health adjustment as compared to high education groups.

- As far as comparison of those males and females who have working status, males in business (as compared to females in business) and females in service (as compared to females in business) show significantly better health adjustment as evident from their means.
- Health adjustment during middle age is not affected by age of marriage since all the calculated 't' are not significant.
- When health adjustment of middle aged males and females from nuclear and joint family is compared, it is evident that health adjustment of male and female from nuclear and joint families is more or less the same, since none of the t value is significant.
- It is also evident from the table that married years do not effect health adjustment of males whereas females in married year group 20-30 show better health adjustment as compared to males of that group and also better from females who are married for more than thirty years. It may be due to the fact that females feel gradual deterioration in their health due to various factors including menopause in later years of middle age.

Demographic factors of home adjustment

H0: There is no significant difference in home adjustment of middle aged males and females with reference to their demographic characteristics.

Table 5: M±SD and t-values for home adjustment of middle aged with reference of demographic variables

S. No.	*Demographic Variables*	*Categories*	*Male (555) Mean± SD*	*Female (555) Mean± SD*	*T-values*
1.	**Age**	50-55 (a)	21.39±3.12	21.06±3.74	.974
		55-60 (b)	21.31±3.48	21.28±4.01	.064
		t-values (a) (b)	.269	.485	
2.	**Education**	Illiterate to primary (a)	22.53±2.87	21.93±3.20	1.95
		Matriculation to higher secondary (b)	20.51±3.70	20.48±4.01	.076
		Graduation and above (c)	21.11±3.22	20.20±4.23	. 2.21*
		t-values (a) (b)	5.55*	4.18*	

(Contd...)

		t-values (b) (c)	1.73	.566	
		t-values (a) (c)	4.41*	4.38*	
3.	**Occupation**	Jobs / Service (a)	21.40±3.33	20.00±4.83	2.17*
		Business (b)	21.46±3.20	18.50±3.42	2.55*
		t-values (a) (b)	.202	.824	
4.	**Age at the time of marriage**	Below18-21 (a)	21.35±3.39	21.26±3.69	.244
		21-30 (b)	21.28±3.43	20.81±3.94	1.50
		Above 30 (c)	22.16±2.14	19.50±3.53	1.59
		t-values (a) (b)	1.00	1.34	
		t-values (b) (c)	1.09	.468	
		t-values (a) (c)	1.00	.674	
5.	**Type of family**	Nuclear (a)	21.24±3.31	20.81±3.96	1.53
		Joint (b)	21.47±3.50	21.56±3.41	.252
		t-values (a) (b)	.793	2.27*	
6.	**Married years**	20-30 (a)	21.25±3.18	19.53±4.68	4.22*
		30-40 (b)	21.37±3.49	21.30±3.70	.279
		t-values (a) (b)	..385	4.85	

Analysis and Interpretation: when compared for home adjustments of middle age with different demographical factors above table indicated following facts:

- No significant difference in t ratio for males and females in both the age group indicate that home adjustment of middle aged males and of females of different age group is more or less same.
- Although in all the three education categories mean value of males is higher than females but this is not significant except for graduation and above group. High educated males show better home adjustment than females of that group as far as adjustment of three educational groups of males and females are concerned. But home adjustment of less educated group is better than higher educated group for both males as well as females.
- When compared on the basis of occupation, males in jobs as well as business have better home adjustment than females in jobs and business but mean in home adjustment of within the occupation group is more or less same.
- Age at the time of marriage do not effect home adjustment of males and females
- In general there is no significant difference in home adjustment of males and females of nuclear and joint family. But within female group home adjustment of females of joint family is better than nuclear family females.

- Married years do not affect home adjustment of males (t not significant). Between 20-30 married years group, home adjustment of males is better than females but in group 30-40 married years, home adjustment of females improved considerably and at par with males of that group.

Demographic factors of social adjustment

H0: There is no significant difference in social adjustment of middle aged males and females with reference to their demographic characteristics.

Table 6: M±SD and t-values for social adjustment of middle aged with reference of demographic variables

S. No.	*Demographic Variables*	*Categories*	*Male Mean± SD*	*Female Mean± SD*	*T-values*
1.	**Age**	50-55 (a)	16.:15±3.03	16.13±3.25	.063
		55-60 (b)	16.37±2.74	16.21±2.96	.480
		t-values (a) (b)	.794	.199	
2.	**Education**	Illiterate to primary (a)	16.72±2.48	16.39.2.82	1.22
		Matriculation to higher secondary (b)	15.92±2.94	15.91±3.17	.001
		Graduation and above (c)	16.33±2.92	15.95±3.94	.994
		t-values (a) (b)	2.71*	1.64	
		t-values (b) (c)	1.38	.084	
		t-values (a) (c)	1.39	1.24	
3.	**Occupation**	Jobs / Service (a)	16.32±2.93	16.75±3.78	.769
		Business (b)	16.32±2.58	14.75±3.99	1.64
		t-values (a) (b)	.007	1.32	
4.	**Age at the time of marriage**	Below18-21 (a)	16.24±2.991	6.27±2.97	.072
		21-30 (b)	16.32±2.80	15.91±3.59	1.52
		Above 30 (c)	16.53±2.17	17.50±3.53	.579
		t-values (a) (b)	.395	1.23	
		t-values (b) (c)	.316	.622	
		t-values (a) (c)	.395	.585	
5.	**Type of family**	Nuclear (a)	16.32±2.73	16.07±3.42	1.06
		Joint (b)	16.29±2.97	16.26±2.82	.084
		t-values (a) (b)	.155	.678	
6.	**Married years**	20-30 (a)	16.23±2.72	20.73±3.91	13.09*
		30-40 (b)	16.35±2.87	16.25±3.03	.465
		t-values (a) (b)	.499	14.92*	

Analysis and Interpretation: when compared for social adjustments of middle age with different demographical factors above table indicated following facts:

- Age, occupation, age at the time of marriage and type of family do not affect social adjustment of middle aged males and females.
- But as evident from the above table social adjustment of less educated group is better than higher educated group and lowest in matriculation to high secondary education group but this difference is significantly higher for illiterate to primary education group males and indicates better social adjustment of that group.
- Similarly females in married to 20-30 years group show better social adjustment than other groups. It may be due to the fact that their roles change and they get less time for socialization and other activities.

Demographic factors of marital adjustment

H0: There is no significant difference in marital adjustment of middle aged males and females with reference to their demographic characteristics.

Table 7: M±SD and t-values for marital adjustment of middle aged with reference of demographic variables

S. No.	*Demographic Variables*	*Categories*	*Male Mean± SD*	*Female Mean± SD*	*T-values*
1.	**Age**	50-55 (a)	14.03±1.85	13.66±2.42	1.74
		55-60 (b)	13.84±2.36	13.74±2.	12 .337
		t-values (a) (b)	.919	.313	
2.	**Education**	Illiterate to primary (a)	14.25±1.59	14.00±2.01	1.35
		Matriculation to higher secondary (b)	13.61±2.23	13.40±2.34	.850
		Graduation and above (c)	13.85±2.58	13.35±3.02	1.59
		t-values (a) (b)	2.99*	2.82*	
		t-values (b) (c)	.988	.161	
		t-values (a) (c)	1.71 2	.44*	
3.	**Occupation**	Jobs / Service (a)	13.88±2.10	13.75±2.71	.313
		Business (b)	14.00±2.39	12.50±2.26	1.73
		t-values (a) (b)	.626	1.20	
4.	**Age at the time of marriage**	Below18-21 (a)	13.67±2.19	13.73±2.25	.267
		21-30 (b)	13.93±2.27	13.57±2.60	1.77
		Above 30 (c)	14.42±1.46	13.00±1.41	1.30
		t-values (a) (b)	1.44	.778	
		t-values (b) (c)	.924	.306	
		t-values (a) (c)	1.44	.458	

(Contd...)

5.	**Type of family**	Nuclear (a)	13.94±2.23	13.58±2.47	1.94
		Joint (b)	13.81±2.24	13.81±2.21	.022
		t-values (a) (b)	.648	1.07	
6.	**Married years**	20-30 (a)	13.95±1.96	15.95±3.51	6.90*
		30-40 (b)	13.86±2.36	13.72±2.20	.813
		t-values (a) (b)	.447 9	.15*	

Analysis and Interpretation: when compared for marital adjustments of middle age with different demographical factors above table indicated following facts:

- Age, occupation, age at the time of marriage and type of family do not affect marital adjustment of middle aged males and females.
- Marital adjustment of illiterate to primary group (males as well as females) is better than other two education groups.
- Marital adjustment of females married for 20 -30 years is highest and better than other groups of males and females and declines as they grow.
- Males and females living in nuclear family adjustment reported more or less same in marital adjustment.

Demographic factors of emotional adjustment

H0: There is no significant difference in emotional adjustment of middle aged males and females with reference to their demographic characteristics.

Table 8: M±SD and t-values for emotional adjustment of middle aged with reference of demographic variables

S. No.	*Demographic Variables*	*Categories*	*Male Mean± SD*	*Female Mean± SD*	*T-values*
1.	**Age**	50-55 (a)	15.83±3.51	15.53±3.77	.867
		55-60 (b)	16.00±3.13	15.64±3.01	.989
		t-values (a) (b)	.554	.252	
2.	**Education**	Illiterate to primary (a)	16.38±2.79	15.82±3.60	1.69
		Matriculation to higher secondary (b)	15.50±3.47	15.42±3.40	.209
		Graduation and above (c)	16.02±3.30	15.15±4.13	2.11*
		t-values (a) (b)	2.55*	1.14	
		t-values (b) (c)	1.53	.610	
		t-values (a) (c)	1.11 1	.58	
3.	**Occupation**	Jobs / Service (a)	16.13±3.19	15.94±3.88	.321

(Contd...)

		Business (b)	15.83±3.18	12.00±5.34 3	.23*
		t-values (a) (b)	1.04 2	.37*	
4.	**Age at the time of marriage**	Below18-21 (a)	15.98±3.22	15.71±3.54	.754
		21-30 (b)	15.97±3.25	15.81±3.87	2.49*
		Above 30 (c)	15.63±3.14	18.50±.707	1.25
		t-values (a) (b)	.445	1.53	
		t-values (b) (c)	.439	1.19	
		t-values (a) (c)	.445	1.11	
5.	**Type of family**	Nuclear (a)	15.87±3.37	15.40±3.72	1.74
		Joint (b)	16.09±3.00	15.78±3.58	.967
		t-values (a) (b)	.777	1.19	
6.	**Married years**	20-30 (a)	15.99±3.44	13.58±2.68	7.69*
		30-40 (b)	15.94±3.12	15.66±3.56	1.10
		t-values (a) (b)	.193	7.12*	

Analysis and Interpretation: when compared for emotional adjustments of middle age with different demographical factors above table indicated following facts:

- It seems that emotional adjustment of males is better than females for all the demographic characteristics but this is significant only for education, occupation, age at the time of marriage and married years. Age and type of family do not affect emotional adjustment of middle aged males and females.
- In high educated group there is significant difference between two sexes and males show better emotional adjustment. Strangely low education groups illiterate to primary, show better emotional adjustment than other groups in males as well as females.
- Males in business reported significantly better emotional adjustment than females in business group. Whereas, females in jobs/services report significantly better emotional adjustment than females in business.
- Males and females married in 20-30 years group show significant difference in emotional adjustment, males displaying better emotional adjustment but in 30-40 years married group it is at par in males and females. It indicates that by the advancement of married years females gradually show better emotional adjustment.

Demographic factors of financial adjustment

H0: There is no significant difference in financial adjustment of middle aged males and females with reference to their demographic characteristics.

Table 9: M±SD and t-values for financial adjustment of middle aged with reference of demographic variables

S. No.	*Demographic Variables*	*Categories*	*Male Mean± SD*	*Female Mean± SD*	*T-values*
1.	**Age**	50-55 (a)	9.77±1.86	9.46±2.12	1.59
		55-60 (b)	9.89±1.85	9.87±1.88	.099
		t-values (a) (b)	.680	1.66	
2.	**Education**	Illiterate to primary (a)	10.01±1.58	9.70±1.89	1.72
		Matriculation to higher secondary (b)	9.71±1.97	9.4±2.17	1.77
		Graduation and above (c)	9.87±1.92	9.45±2.34	1.75
		t-values (a) (b)	1.53	1.96*	
		t-values (b) (c)	.810	.509	
		t-values (a) (c)	.756	1.10	
3.	**Occupation**	Jobs / Service (a)	9.92±1.80	10.00±2.35	.225
		Business (b)	9.77±1.93	8.25±1.98	2.18*
		t-values (a) (b)	.920	1.93	
4.	**Age at the time of marriage**	Below18-21 (a)	9.76±1.79	9.52±2.02	1.14
		21-30 (b)	9.78±1.88	9.52±2.22	2.01*
		Above 30 (c)	10.47±1.57	11.50±.707	.895
		t-values (a) (b)	1.65	.046	
		t-values (b) (c)	1.38	1.25	
		t-values (a) (c)	1.65	1.38	
5.	**Type of family**	Nuclear (a)	9.85±1.82	9.45±2.16	2.60*
		Joint (b)	9.88±1.90	9.65±1.97	1.22
		t-values (a) (b)	.214	1.10	
6.	**Married years**	20-30 (a)	9.89±1.82	15.33±3.85	17.73*
		30-40 (b)	9.85±1.86	9.60±2.00	1.70
		t-values (a) (b)	.278	23.05*	

Analysis and Interpretation: when compared for financial adjustments of middle age with different demographical factors above table indicated following facts:

- There is no significant difference in financial adjustment of middle age males and females of different age groups.
- Same is true for financial adjustment of middle aged males and females from different educational status, strangely less educated group show better financial adjustment (but not significant).
- Although females in service show better financial adjustment than males but this different is not significant, whereas males in business show significantly better financial adjustment than business women.

- Age of marriage is not associated with financial adjustment of middle aged males and females as mean differences are not significant.
- Financial adjustment of nuclear family males is better than females but this difference is not significant for joint family males and females.
- 20-30 married years group females show better financial adjustment than 30-40 year group and even better than males of two groups. It is lowest in females of 30-40 years married group, may be due to the fact that expenses go on increasing and women have to take care of needs of growing children and sometimes also for old age in-laws and for their own expenses.

Conclusion: It is evident from the above analysis that Adjustment; health, home, social, marital, emotional and financial is better for low educated group, may be because of less demands, more compromising situations and low expectations to maintain standards. In term s of age, it is seen that couple's age does not affect adjustments, because till middle age they have already spent much time together and become well adjusted. Males reported better health, home, emotional, financial adjustments in business category than females whereas, females having better health, home, emotional, financial adjustment in job/service category. Males, who got married between 21-30 year age, reported better emotional and financial adjustment, because it is believed to be ideal age for males to be married, when they are financially independent and emotionally matured. Depending on the type of family it was found that joint family couples are having better home and financial adjustment than nuclear family couples may be because in joint family couples get support from other family members. In couples who are married for 20-30 years, it was found that males show better home and emotional adjustment; whereas, females reported better health, social, marital and financial adjustment.

Part IV: Life Satisfaction of Middle Aged Males and Females

Life satisfaction of middle aged was measured separately for males and females in five areas mental, job, social, marital and family. Raw scores for life satisfaction are given in appendix-VII. Mean, SD values and t ratios were calculated which have been presented in the following table.

H0: There is no significant difference in life satisfaction (mental, job, social, marital and family) among middle aged males and females.

Table 10: M±SD and t-values for life satisfaction of middle aged males and females

S. No.	*Areas of Life Satisfaction*	*Male (555) Mean± SD*	*Female (555) Mean± SD*	*t-values*
1.	Mental	35.57±3.713	35.38±3.938	.863
2.	Job	26.57±6.419	23.01±7.910	8.230*
3.	Social	28.46±4.964	28.14±4.792	1.077
4.	Marital	29.70±3.680	29.75±3.660	.213
5.	Family	16.97±1.708	17.01±1.749	.347

* Significant

As evident from the above table, out of the five areas of life satisfaction t values for only one satisfaction area; job is significant. It indicates significant difference in job satisfaction of males and females. Higher mean score of males depict that job satisfaction of males is better than females. Reason may be that males are employed and free to take decisions, whereas most of the females are not in paid jobs.

In other areas mental, social, marital and family, life satisfaction is more or less same.

Part V: Demographic Factors of Life Satisfaction in Middle Aged Males and Females

To find out differences in life satisfaction with demographic variables under study, Mean± SD and t calculated for males and females have been presented in the tables below, separately for each area of life satisfaction; mental , job, social, marital and financial.

Demographic factors of mental satisfaction

H0: There is no significant difference in mental satisfaction of middle aged males and females with reference to their demographic characteristics.

Table 11: M±SD and t-values for mental satisfaction among middle aged with reference of demographic variables

S. No.	*Demographic Variables*	*Categories*	*Male Mean± SD*	*Female Mean± SD*	*T-values*
1.	**Age**	50-55 (a)	35.45±4.00	35.44±3.90	.009
		55-60 (b)	35.62±3.60	35.01±4.10	1.39
		t-values (a) (b)	.494	.935	

(Contd...)

2.	**Education**	Illiterate to primary (a)	35.74±3.32	35.65±3.58	.261
		Matriculation to higher secondary (b)	35.77±3.52	35.81±4.40	.227*
		Graduation and above (c)	35.29±4.11	35.63±3.90	.731
		t-values (a) (b)	.098	2.18*	
		t-values (b) (c)	1.23	1.64	
		t-values (a) (c)	1.12	.039	
3.	**Occupation**	Jobs / Service (a)	35.72±3.84	36.66±3.98	1.30
		Business (b)	35.49±3.38	35.00±4.98	.395
		t-values (a) (b)	.696	1.00	
4.	**Age at the time of marriage**	Below18-21 (a)	35.23±3.92	35.21±3.94	.052
		21-30 (b)	35.65±3.66	35.68±3.91	.095
		Above 30 (c)	36.21±3.29	35.50±6.36	.271
		t-values (a) (b)	1.12	1.36	
		t-values (b) (c)	.651	.066	
		t-values (a) (c)	1.03	.105	
5.	**Type of family**	Nuclear (a)	35.34±3.82	35.37±3.88	.129
		Joint (b)	35.96±3.50	35.38±4.03	1.57
		t-values (a) (b)	1.92	.017	
6.	**Married years**	20-30 (a)	35.57±3.81	35.82±3.90	.633
		30-40 (b)	35.58±3.66	35.14±3.94	1.54
		t-values (a) (b)	.022	1.93	

Analysis and Interpretation: when compared for mental satisfaction of middle age with different demographical factors above table indicated following facts:

- Since all the t calculated for mental satisfaction within male and female groups and between males and female groups are non significant, for all demographic variables hence it may be concluded that mental satisfaction is independent of demographic characteristic of respondents.

Demographic factors of job satisfaction

H0: There is no significant difference in job satisfaction of middle aged males and females with reference to their demographic characteristics.

Table 12: M±SD and t-values for job satisfaction among middle aged with reference of demographic variables

S. No.	*Demographic Variables*	*Categories*	*Male Mean± SD*	*Female Mean± SD*	*T-values*
1.	**Age**	50-55 (a)	26.31±6.24	23.04±7.86	4.64*
		55-60 (b)	26.66±6.48	22.80±8.17	4.76*
		t-values (a) (b)	.564	.261	
2.	**Education**	Illiterate to primary (a)	25.12±6.16	22.93±7.14	3.21*
		Matriculation to higher secondary (b)	27.07±6.35	23.63±8.45	4.32*
		Graduation and above (c)	27.22±6.51	22.26±8.65	5.92*
		t-values (a) (b)	2.86*	.937	
		t-values (b) (c)	.218	1.35	
		t-values (a) (c)	3.16*	.788	
3.	**Occupation**	Jobs / Service (a)	26.23±6.66	24.66±8.21	1.25
		Business (b)	26.90±5.92	27.50±5.68	.282
		t-values (a) (b)	1.15	.921	
4.	**Age at the time of marriage**	Below18-21 (a)	26.31±6.46	22.98±7.65	4.38*
		21-30 (b)	26.53±6.45	23.06±8.34	5.61*
		Above 30 (c)	28.95±4.99	22.00±15.55	1.55
		t-values (a) (b)	.332	.111	
		t-values (b) (c)	1.60	.178	
		t-values (a) (c)	1.69	.180	
5.	**Type of family**	Nuclear (a)	26.78±6.44	23.00±7.95	6.83*
		Joint (b)	26.22±6.37	23.02±7.85	4.60*
		t-values (a) (b)	1.01	.038	
6.	**Married years**	20-30 (a)	27.06±6.30	23.22±8.01	5.22*
		30-40 (b)	26.30±6.47	22.89±7.86	6.37*
		t-values (a) (b)	1.31	.469	

Analysis and Interpretation: when compared for job satisfaction of middle age with different demographical factors above table indicated following facts:

When compared job satisfaction of males and females within their age groups there is no significant difference but in both the age groups job satisfaction of males is higher than females of that age group.

- As far as education and job satisfaction is concerned, among males group there is significant difference and high educated males report significantly better job satisfaction than low education groups but this trend is not observed in female groups. Job satisfaction of females in three education groups is more or less same. But when compared among males and females of three education levels this difference is significant and higher for males.

- Job satisfaction is not affected by type of occupation and more or less same for males and females of service or business groups.
- There is significant difference in job satisfaction of males and females with reference to type of family, age of marriage and married years and job satisfaction is higher among males.
- It may be due to the fact that more males are in job and better paid than females and have more freedom to decide upon financial matters.

Demographic factors of social satisfaction

H0: There is no significant difference in social satisfaction of middle aged males and females with reference to their demographic characteristics.

Table 13: M±SD and t-values for social satisfaction among middle aged with reference of demographic variables

S. No.	*Demographic Variables*	*Categories*	*Male Mean± SD*	*Female Mean± SD*	*T-values*
1.	**Age**	50-55 (a)	28.09±5.38	28.29±4.59	.428
		55-60 (b)	28.59±4.79	27.35±5.72	2.10*
		t-values (a) (b)	1.04	1.66	
2.	**Education**	Illiterate to primary (a)	27.37±4.68	27.60±4.77	.478
		Matriculation to higher secondary (b)	28.75±4.91	28.31±4.91	.839
		Graduation and above (c)	29.01±5.09	29.08±4.53	.111
		t-values (a) (b)	2.63*	1.52	
		t-values (b) (c)	.517	1.35	
		t-values (a) (c)	3.20*	2.84*	
3.	**Occupation**	Jobs / Service (a)	28.35±5.17	28.25±4.68	.106
		Business (b)	28.33±4.72	29.12±4.22	.469
		t-values (a) (b)	.051	.481	
4.	**Age at the time of marriage**	Below18-21 (a)	28.20±5.14	27.96±4.68	.496
		21-30 (b)	28.53±4.90	28.41±4.96	.274
		Above 30 (c)	28.53±5.09	34.00±1.41	1.48
		t-values (a) (b)	.646	1.07	
		t-values (b) (c)	.004	1.58	
		t-values (a) (c)	.254	1.82	

(Contd...)

5.	**Type of family**	Nuclear (a)	28.51±4.95	28.35±4.89	.412
		Joint (b)	28.37±4.99	27.80±4.61	1.23
		t-values (a) (b)	.318	1.32	
6.	**Married years**	20-30 (a)	28.90±4.92	28.56±4.87	.675
		30-40 (b)	28.22±4.97	27.91±4.73	.842
		t-values (a) (b)	1.54	1.52	

Analysis and Interpretation: when compared for social satisfaction of middle age with different demographical factors above table indicated following facts:

- As evident from the above table, in younger age group middle age males and females have same level of social satisfaction, but in later years of middle age, males show better social satisfaction than females.
- Social satisfaction among middle age female is not affected by their education level and more or less same for all the three categories whereas in middle age males it is highest in higher educated group and lowest in low education group.
- There is no significant difference in social satisfaction among middle aged male and female with reference to type of occupation, age of marriage, type of family and married years.

Demographic factors of marital satisfaction

H0: There is no significant difference in marital satisfaction of middle aged males and females with reference to their demographic characteristics.

Table 14: M±SD and t-values for marital satisfaction among middle aged with reference of demographic variables:

S. No.	*Demographic Variables*	*Categories*	*Male Mean± SD*	*Female Mean± SD*	*T-values*
1.	**Age**	50-55 (a)	29.79±3.42	29.78±3.62	.039
		55-60 (b)	29.67±3.77	29.59±3.85	.175
		t-values (a) (b)	.346	.436	
2.	**Education**	Illiterate to primary (a)	28.84±3.43	29.26±3.43	1.19
		Matriculation to higher secondary (b)	29.76±3.63	30.25±3.62	1.27
		Graduation and above (c)	30.29±3.78	30.09±4.04	.455
		t-values (a) (b)	2.36*	2.89*	
		t-values (b) (c)	1.42	.349	
		t-values (a) (c)	3.82*	2.07*	

(Contd...)

3.	**Occupation**	Jobs / Service (a)	29.74±3.62	30.59±4.11	1.25
		Business (b)	29.55±3.76	29.50±4.27	.039
		t-values (a) (b)	.575	.668	
4.	**Age at the time of marriage**	Below18-21 (a)	29.59±3.57	29.62±3.68	.090
		21-30 (b)	229.75±3.68	29.95±3.62	.646
		Above 30 (c)	29.53±4.38	32.50±.707	.936
		t-values (a) (b)	.424	1.01	
		t-values (b) (c)	..254	.989	
		t-values (a) (c)	.071	1.10	
5.	**Type of family**	Nuclear (a)	29.87±3.73	29.91±3.54	.147
		Joint (b)	29.44±3.58	29.49±3.82	.157
		t-values (a) (b)	1.35	1.31	
6.	**Married years**	20-30 (a)	29.65±3.72	29.76±3.65	.290
		30-40 (b)	29.73±3.65	29.75±3.66	.051
		t-values (a) (b)	.265	.024	

Analysis and Interpretation: when compared for marital satisfaction of middle age with different demographical factors above table indicated following facts:

- It seems that education is an important demographic characteristic for married life satisfaction among middle aged males and females. Less educated middle aged couples (males as well as females) show poor marital satisfaction than other two education groups.
- All other demographic characteristics- age, occupation, age of marriage, type of family and married years do not affect marital satisfaction during middle age.

Demographic factors of family satisfaction

H0: There is no significant difference in family satisfaction of middle aged males and females with reference to their demographic characteristics.

Table 15: M±SD and t-values for family satisfaction among middle aged with reference of demographic variables:

S. No.	*Demographic Variables*	*Categories*	*Male Mean± SD*	*Female Mean± SD*	*T-values*
1.	**Age**	50-55 (a)	17.09±1.51	17.07±1.65	.107
		55-60 (b)	16.93±1.77	16.67±2.15	1.17
		t-values (a) (b)	.954	1.93	
2.	**Education**	Illiterate to primary (a)	17.27±1.44	17.07±1.66	1.25
		Matriculation to higher secondary (b)	16.90±1.75	16.98±1.83	.414

(*Contd...*)

		Graduation and above (c)	16.81±1.82	16.92±1.81	.501
		t-values (a) (b)	2.07* .	510	
		t-values (b) (c)	.507	.309	
		t-values (a) (c)	2.61* .	809	
3.	**Occupation**	Jobs / Service (a)	16.95±1.69	16.69±1.87	.829
		Business (b)	17.03±1.75	15.75±2.49	1.98*
		t-values (a) (b)	.494*	1.18	
4.	**Age at the time of marriage**	Below18-21 (a)	16.98±1.89	16.98±1.79	.006
		21-30 (b)	16.96±1.66	17.06±1.67	.675
		Above 30 (c)	17.26±1.44	18.00±.000	.704
		t-values (a) (b)	. 103	.504	
		t-values (b) (c)	.786	.794	
		t-values (a) (c)	.632	.806	
5.	**Type of family**	Nuclear (a)	16.95±1.71	16.97±1.81	.130
		Joint (b)	17.01±1.70	17.08±1.64	.405
		t-values (a) (b)	.396	.702	
6.	**Married years**	20-30 (a)	29.65±3.72	29.76±3.65	.290
		30-40 (b)	16.96±1.69	16.98±1.76	.172
		t-values (a) (b)	.220	.472	

Analysis and Interpretation: when compared for family satisfaction of middle age with different demographical factors above table indicated following facts:

- Out of the t calculated for family satisfaction of middle age males and females only education and occupation categories show signi ficant differences.
- Males in low education group (illiterate to primary) show better family life satisfaction than other two educated groups of males but this is not significant for females.
- Males and females in jobs are more or less equal in their family satisfaction but males in business show better mean score for family satisfaction than females in business.
- For all other demographical characteristic family satisfaction of middle aged males and females does not differ significantly.

Conclusion: Males reported better job and social satisfaction than females with respect to age variable. The reason might be because males are having more extrovert personality than females in this age, so have more outdoor interaction and activities.

Life satisfaction patterns are different for different educational background. Couples educated in illiterate to primary category reported better family satisfaction whereas matriculation to higher secondary studied couples have better mental satisfaction. However, graduation and above educated couples have better job, social and marital satisfaction.

Working men reported better family satisfaction than working women. The reason might be that women also have to handle household responsibilities apart from their occupational work responsibilities. Males from nuclear and joint family report better job satisfaction than females. Because males in mid-age are better able to handle job and get better satisfaction in it than females. The similar satisfaction pattern is found for couples married years wherein, males are having better job satisfaction than female.

Part VI: Association Between Adjustment of Husband and Wife

Pearson correlations have been calculated to find out relationship between adjustment of husband and wife which has been presented in the table below- Critical value of r to be significant at .05 level is 0.088.

H0: There is no significant relationship between adjustment of middle aged husband and wife.

Table 16: Correlation between adjustment of husband and wife

S. No.	*Adjustment Areas Husband Wife*	*Health*	*Home*	*Social*	*Marital*	*Emotional*	*Financial*
1.	Health	.503*	.409*	.366*	.309*	.351*	.225*
2.	Home	.437*	.584*	.443*	.378*	.349*	.314*
3.	Social	.405*	.456*	.563*	.319*	.354*	.235*
4.	Marital	.299*	.383*	.335*	.462*	.236*	.123*
5.	Emotional	.398*	.369*	.380*	.213*	.544*	.273*
6.	Financial	.302*	.358*	.311*	.164*	.334*	.489*

* Significant

The result shows that there is significant correlation between health, home, social, marital, emotional and financial adjustment of husband and wife. Since all the correlation values are positive it may be inferred that good or poor adjustment of one spouse leads to good or poor adjustment of the other. Poor adjustment in one area may also lead to poor adjustment in other areas of adjustment.

Part VI: Association Between Life Satisfaction of Husband and Wife

Following table shows correlation values for different areas of life satisfaction between middle aged husband and wife.

H0: There is no significant relationship between life satisfaction among middle aged husband and wife.

Table 17: Correlation between life satisfaction of husband and wife

S. No.	*Life Satisfaction Areas Husband Wife*	*Mental*	*Job*	*Social*	*Marital*	*Family*
1.	Mental	529*	.177*	.158*	.144*	.342*
2.	Job	.319*	.289*	.223*	.177*	.231*
3.	Social	.196*	.485*	.537*	.431*	.185*
4.	Marital	.040	.382*	.403*	.566*	.264*
5.	Family	.228*	.169*	.142*	.227*	.524*

* Significant

The results show that there is positive and significant correlation between life satisfaction in all the areas i.e. mental, job, social, marital and family. All but one r values are more than critical value show significance of correlation and interrelation of different areas of life satisfaction. Low or high satisfaction in one area may precipitate in low or high satisfaction in another area. Likewise low or high life satisfaction of one spouse may lead to low or high life satisfaction in other better half.

Part VII: Association Between Adjustment and Life Satisfaction of Middle Aged Males and Females

Males

The following table shows correlation values between adjustment areas (health, home, social, marital, emotional and financial) and life satisfaction areas (mental, job social, marital and family) of middle aged males.

H0: There is no significant relationship between adjustment and life satisfaction of middle aged couples.

Table 18: Correlation between adjustment and life satisfaction of middle aged males

S. No.	*Adjustment Areas* *Life satisfaction Areas*	*Health*	*Home*	*Social*	*Marital*	*Emotional*	*Financial*
1.	Mental	.143*	.201*	.195*	.029	.160*	.140*
2.	Job	-.065	-.078	.056	-.020	.108*	-.066
3.	Social	-.081	-.130*	-.008	-.038	.040	-.145*
4.	Marital	-.079	-.146*	-.031	-.023	.055	-.060
5.	Family	.188*	.203*	.214*	.112*	.151*	.120*

* Significant at the 0.05 level

As evident from above table adjustment and life satisfaction in various areas are related with each other, positive with some areas and negative in other areas.

- Mental satisfaction among middle aged male is significantly associated with their health, home, social, emotional and financial adjustment which indicate that better health, home, social, emotional and financial adjustment leads to higher mental satisfaction among middle aged males.
- Although job satisfaction is positively related with emotional adjustment and negatively related with health, home, marital and financial adjustment but only one r value (job with emotional adjustment) is significant. Greater job satisfaction leads to better emotional adjustment or vice versa.
- Social satisfaction is negatively and significantly correlated with home and financial adjustment. Better home and financial adjustment may hinder with social life satisfaction. Since calculated values for all other areas of adjustment i.e. health, social, marital and emotional are not significant it helps to conclude that these areas of adjustment are independent of social life satisfaction.
- Only one value of correlation between marital satisfaction and home adjustment is significant but negative. Better home adjustment may sometimes precipitate in lower marital satisfaction. It reveals that good Adjustment did not guarantee a better life satisfaction in some areas.

Family life satisfaction show positive and significant association with all the areas of adjustment - health, home, social, marital, emotional and financial which indicates that better adjustment in all spheres provide higher family life satisfaction among middle aged males.

Females

The table below shows correlation values between life satisfaction and adjustment of middle aged females in various areas.

Table 19: Correlation between adjustment and life satisfaction of middle aged females

S. No.	***Adjustment Areas*** ***Life satisfaction Areas***	***Health***	***Home***	***Social***	***Marital***	***Emotional***	***Financial***
1.	Mental	137*	.180*	.235*	.120*	.237*	.120*
2.	Job	.058	.012	.111*	.012	.102*	.085*
3.	Social	-.153*	-.101*	-.012	-.054	.033	-.120*
4.	Marital	-.134*	-.072	.015	-.008	.045	-.050
5.	Family	.117*	.229*	.224*	.161*	.160*	.098*

* Significant at the 0.05 level

As evident from the table above-

- Mental satisfaction is positively and significantly associated with all the areas of adjustment -health, home, social, marital, emotional and financial adjustments. This means better adjustment positively affects mental satisfaction of middle aged females.
- Job satisfaction is positively correlated with social, emotional and financial adjustments. This indicates that greater job satisfaction allows better social, emotional and financial adjustments. It may be due to the fact that when women are financially sound they have more say in financial matters , may spend more money as per their wish and get more social acceptance which leads to better job life satisfaction.
- It is strange to note that social satisfaction is negatively correlated with health, home and financial adjustment. More socializing may provide greater social satisfaction but may be the cause of poor home adjustment, more financial burden and sometimes poor health.
- Out of calculated r values of marital satisfaction with various areas of adjustment only one value that is with health adjustment is significant, but inverse. It helps to conclude that better marital satisfaction may be the cause of poor health adjustment. In case of middle aged women more demands on marital responsibilities, pressure to perform better may take its toll on their health.
- Similar to middle aged males, Family satisfaction is positively and significantly associated with health, home, social, marital,

emotional and financial adjustment areas. When women are overall adjusted to different areas in life they get more family life satisfaction.

Part VIII: Factors of Adjustment And Satisfaction in Middle Adulthood

How daily frequency of family stressors affect life may be an interesting aspect of research, which motivated the investigator to find out perception of middle aged couples about factors of influence for adjustment and life satisfaction. As mentioned in earlier chapter, researcher developed a check list based on research findings, pilot study and opinions of experts to seek opinion of couples on parameters which can adversely effect adjustment and life satisfaction during middle age in family settings.

These factors have been divided in five parameters- Physical illness and chronic disease (14 items), Mental health (16 items), Positive thinking and Decision making (16 items), Relation with life partner (20 items) and Family environment (15 items).Yes responses of couples for each item, presented in frequency (of response) and listed in order of ranking (factors given most often to least by middle aged couples) separately for middle aged men and women for each parameter in have been presented in the following tables.

Table 20: Physical illness and chronic disease related factors of adjustment and life satisfaction given by middle aged men and women

Men	Women
Declining physical strength (296)	Declining physical strength (293)
Huge expenses on medicines (261)	Huge expenses on medicines (244)
Increased dependency on family members (173)	Increased dependency on family members (177)
Desire to eat peppery and spicy (due to continuous abstinence or regulated diet) (142)	Often need assistance of others(145)
Inability to meet needs of family members (141)	Desire to eat peppery and spicy (due to continuous abstinence or regulated diet) (133)
Responsibility of caring for sick family member (130)	Inability to meet needs of family members (133)
Inability to meet the household expenses due to illness (128)	Responsibility of caring for sick family member(123)

(*Contd...*)

Often need assistance of others(123)	Inability to meet the household expenses due to illness (109)
Fulfill social responsibilities because of alone to illness engagement of spouse (117)	Inability to help family in house hold chores (96)
Inability to help family in house hold chores (98)	Fulfill social responsibilities because of alone to illness engagement of spouse (92)
Dismissive behaviour of family members (93)	Dismissive behaviour of family members (91)
Changes in routines due to illness of family member (76)	Family members considering as helpless(73)
Family members considering as helpless(61)	Changes in routines due to incurable illness of family member (72)
House mates talk complaining (55)	House mates talk complaining (61)

Since middle age can bring on new health problems and unfortunately the attitude of both care providers and family members, as well as middle aged people too often, show some stereotypical and negative attitudes which can take the form of avoidance, dislike, and begrudged tolerance which might lower adjustment and life satisfaction.

As evident from the table above-

Declining physical strength, huge expenses on medicines and increased dependency on family members are the most important factors related to physical illness and chronic disease during middle age adjustment and life satisfaction since men and women gave highest and similar ranks. Some other factors to lower adjustment and life satisfaction reported are-desire to eat peppery and spicy (may be due to abstinence or regulated diet), inability to meet needs of family members. Middle age people may have to become care givers to ailing/aging parents or other family members which can be source of considerable stress as, evident from the responses of middle aged males, whereas dependency on others for assist once, as reported by females, can lower their adjustment. Least importance was given to continuous complaining of family members, show of feeling of helplessness towards them and change in routine.

Table 21: Mental health related factors of adjustment and life satisfaction given by middle aged men and women

Men	Women
Excessive thinking on any issue(281)	Excessive thinking on any issue(277)
Lack of the enthusiasm as before (239)	Inability to keep calm in routine chores (219)
Inability to keep calm in routine chores (208)	Lack of the enthusiasm as before (214)
Excessive worry (199)	Excessive worry (178)
Getting angrier than before (127)	Irritation / annoyance (117)
Inability to admit mistakes (120)	Dull life (99)
Dull life (112)	Lay differences in the heart (98)
Irritation / annoyance (107)	Getting angrier than before (97)
Lack of tuning in thoughts(105)	Lack of tuning in thoughts(93)
Lay differences in the heart (90)	Inability to admit mistakes (86)
Always feared something bad (74)	Always feared something bad (79)
Always having negative thoughts (62)	Always having negative thoughts (73)
Exaggerated view for small problems (61)	Exaggerated view for small problems (68)
Feeling life futile or meaningless (59)	To be remorse on failed to give the family time (67)
To be remorse on failed to give the family time (56)	Feeling life futile or meaningless (52)
Habit of dissension (24)	Habit of dissension (28)

A good mental health is essential for balanced temperament and calm nature of a mid-age person. In middle-age, couples feel to be on a never-ending treadmill of fulfilling desires and need s of the family and because of these never-ending responsibilities mental peace of middle-age couples disturbs. Troubled mental health can lead to irritation, anger, sleep deprivation, and other psychological issues along with affecting adjustment and life satisfaction of mid-aged couples.

In mental health category, middle-aged men and women gave high ranks to excessive thinking on any issue, inability to keep calm in routine chores, lack of the enthusiasm as earlier and excessive worry. Some other mental health related factors given by men were increase in anger and not accepting own mistakes whereas irritation/ annoyance were reported as important factors by females which may hinder with the adjustment and life satisfaction. The least important mental health factors perceived by men and women were- habit of dissension and feeling life futile or meaningless.

Table 22: Thinking and decision making related factors of adjustment and life satisfaction given by middle aged men and women

Men	Women
Lack of balance in difficulty (311)	Lack of balance in difficulty (289)
Not valuing opinion of others (201)	Not valuing opinion of others (172)
Regret for wrong decisions (192)	Taking quick decision on based on sentiment(156)
Dependence on family members for facing decision (143)	Regret for wrong decisions (154)
Taking quick decision on based on sentiment(142)	Dependence on family members for facing decision (153)
Thinking too much of past (134)	Inability to find solutions(147)
Have to decide alone (113)	Thinking too much of past (123)
Family members not-acceptances your decisions(111)	Inability to control difficulties (107)
Inability to control difficulties (106)	Family members not-acceptances your decisions(93)
Feeling miserable for unfulfilled wishes in life(101)	Binding to obey the decision of others (82)
Inability to find solutions(100)	Indecisiveness (77)
Indecisiveness (98)	Have to decide alone (73)
Binding to obey the decision of others (86)	Feeling miserable for unfulfilled wishes in life(70)
Not including others in decisions (86)	Not including others in decisions (69)
Sense of injustice due to others(60)	Sense of injustice due to others(67)
Someone else getting credit of your work (50)	Someone else getting credit of your work (57)

Middle-age is a time when an adult has to bear the responsibilities for two different generations. It involves taking several crucial decisions not only for oneself but for the whole family. Sometimes, a person has to take some hard decisions for better future of the family and often involving everyone's suggestion in the decision is very difficult, which may create disagreements in the family members. These eventually affect adjustment and life satisfaction in mid-aged couples. Along with being a good decision maker, one should also keep a balanced thought process. Due to issues from family, health, social or professional platforms, a mid-age person develops negative thinking, which may lead to depression and maladjustment and poor life satisfaction.

As evident from table above lack of balance in difficult situation, not valuing opinion of others, taking quick decision based on sentiment, regret for their own decisions and dependence on family members for taking decision were some of the major factors which can lower adjustment and life satisfaction. Least important factors for lowering adjustment and life satisfaction were- someone else getting credit of your work, not including others in decisions, and sense of injustice due to others.

Table 23: Relation with life partner related factors of adjustment and life satisfaction given by middle aged men and women

Men	Women
Partner always finding faults (84)	Stubborn nature of spouses (103)
Spouse arguing on every issue (81)	Spouse being highly ambitious (68)
Spouse being highly ambitious (79)	Partner always finding faults (67)
Stubborn nature of spouses (66)	Spouse arguing on every issue (66)
Non romantic life partner (65)	Stingy partner (60)
Be highly banned by spouse (63)	Life partner being spendthrift/ lavish (50)
Stingy partner (63)	Spouse holding higher position (47)
Negative partner (62)	Non romantic life partner (43)
Unequal education level of spouse (51)	Spouse indulging in addictions (tobacco, smoking, alcohol) (42)
Spouse repeated by providing sense of inferiority (48)	Higher salary of spouse (43)
Spouse holding higher position (39)	Be highly banned by spouse (35)
Life partner being spendthrift/ lavish (35)	Negative partner (33)
Higher salary of spouse (33)	Unequal education level of spouse (24)
Talking bad of spouse in front of friends and acquaintances (29)	Frequent visit of spouse's friends (22)

(Contd...)

Comparison of spouse with friends and others(28)	Suspicious nature of spouse (20)
Suspicious nature of spouse (24)	Spouse repeated by providing sense of inferiority (20)
Spouse not being good to your family (23)	Comparison of spouse with friends and others(19)
Frequent visit of spouse's friends (20)	Talking bad of spouse in front of friends and acquaintances (19)
Spouse indulging in addictions (tobacco, smoking, alcohol) (17)	Spouse not being good to your family (18)
Harassment and violent behavior of spouse (5)	Harassment and violent behavior of spouse (6)

Until mid-age, all the couples face many ups and down of life together. They raise children, develop social contacts, take care of elderly parents and participate in other activities as a team. This develops a unique companionship and understanding of each other's behaviour, likes and dislike. Some of the normative events of mid life are likely to be stressful for one or both partners. Whenever an individual is under stress there is likely to be ripple effect so that people close to the stressed persons are also affected. The one likely to be most affected is a spouse. Exercise like the one above, provides the way to communicate mutual relationship issues which may be sources of maladjustment leading to dissatisfaction among couples.

Some of the highly ranked factors by men and women in relation with life partner category given were - spouse finding faults of each other, arguing on every issue, highly ambitious and stubborn nature of spouse which lower adjustment and life satisfaction in adverse direction. Some other factors reported by men were nonromantic partner, imposing too many bindings and restrictions, unequal educational status and negative attitude of spouse whereas female emphasized too lavish or spend thrift or too much stringy attitude of spouse holding higher position and addiction of substances like alcohol, tobacco as an important factors of maladjustment.

Strangely harassment and violent behaviour of spouse was the least important factors for maladjustment as perceived by both men and women which indirectly indicates that domestic violence including spousal abuse is a regular phenomenon in families is still one of the accepted behaviour among Indian families.

There may be multiple reason that contribute to continue relationship such as fear of loneliness, pride, shame concern, barriers, low self-steam or combination of all part of these.

Table 24: Family environment related factors of adjustment and life satisfaction given by middle aged men and women

Men	Women
Children living away (156)	Children living away (168)
Lack of tolerance in the family (122)	Rigorous discipline (117)
Frequent arguments and fights in family (109)	Lack of tolerance in the family (117)
No respect in family (89)	No respect in family (87)
Too much differences of opinion in family (82)	Frequent arguments and fights in family (80)
Rigorous discipline (82)	Too much differences of opinion in family (70)
Children not self sufficient up to late age (78)	Children not self sufficient up to late age (69)
The lack of harmony in the family (68)	The lack of harmony in the family (59)
Bad company of children (68)	Bad company of children (52)
Rebellious nature of children (62)	Everybody in the family allowed to arbitrary (52)
Everybody in the family allowed to arbitrary (62)	Rebellious nature of children (49)
Rebellious nature of family members (49)	Rebellious nature of family members (35)
Too many restrictions on children (33)	Too many restrictions on children (32)
Children stay out late into the night (30)	Children stay out late into the night (20)
Children feeling disgrace on your appearance and living standards (22)	Children feeling disgrace on your appearance and living standards (13)

Family is a medium which provides the feeling of joy, happiness and fulfilment in mid-aged couple's life. It keeps them engaged to work for a common goal the betterment of the family. But in many cases, several issues develop either due to the difference in opinions, generation gap, unruly children, non-cooperative behaviour, and scattered family. Due to these issues, family members feel isolation and it might lead to family quarrels also.

Strangely post parental years, when children have left, are among the most stressful and important factor of maladjustment and low satisfaction as given by men and women in contrast with study. This may be due to the Indian family structure where parents expect their children to be living with them and continue giving them more attention than get from others and when children leave they feel miserable and lonely.

Some of the important family related factors reported were lack of tolerance in the family, frequent arguments and fights in family, and no respect in family. Rigorous discipline was one of the factor perceived most important by more women (although given due importance by men also). Some other perceived factors leading to maladjustment were- too much difference of opinions, and lack of harmony. One other factor which may be stress causing and lowering life satisfaction may be nonemployment of children up to late age and sometimes their bad company. Men and women gave similar low ranks to factors- children feeling disgrace on your appearance and living standards, children stay out late into the night, too many restrictions on children, and rebellious nature of family members. This indicates that all the family members living together, cooperation and due respect in the family are major factors which affect adjustment and life satisfaction middle aged.

Chapter - 5

Summary, Conclusion and Suggestions

This chapter Summarizes/major findings, conclusions and suggestions which have been deduced on the basis of analysis and interpretation of data.

Since the last few decades revolutionary changes have been observed in the social configuration of Indian society. These changes have brought changes in the structure, morals and nature of the family also. Therefore family organization and its interpersonal relationships needs a revision and redefinition. With special reference to mid-age, which is specifically the time of transitions in all aspects of life. When couples face many physiological, psychological, social and economic and behavioral changes. They also have to redefine their social responsibilities, managing younger and elder age members, and often referred as age of transition or sandwich-age.

Eventually it may affect adjustment and life-satisfaction of mid-age couples, which plays a significant role not only on their behavior but health, attitude towards family life and other aspects. In this backdrop present research has been taken up to unravel the fact related to midlife, stated as “Correlates of adjustment and life satisfaction among middle aged married couples”.

With the objectives to –

1. To study adjustment pattern of middle aged couples
2. To study life satisfaction among these couples and
3. To identify the correlates of adjustment and life satisfaction among middle aged couples

Research Design

The present study was conducted in Narsinghpur district of, Madhya Pradesh state of India. Purposive sampling technique was used for sample selection. The sample comprised of 555 couples (total N=1110) with age range 50-60 years. General Information Blank, Old Age Adjustment Inventory, Life Satisfaction Scale and Check List on Factors of low Adjustment and Satisfaction in Middle Adulthood were used to collect data were analyzed and interpreted in terms of percentage, mean, standard deviation, t-test and correlation.

Major findings

- In general males were older than females as majority of males were in 55-60 years of age and females in 50-55 years of age.
- The male were more educated than their female counterparts.
- Ninety two percent of females were not in paid job and out of those working very few had their own business.
- Age of males was more at the time of marriage as compared to females.
- More couples were from nuclear families but joint family systems were also quite prevalent (thirty eight percent).
- As far as the religion of couples was concerned higher were Hindu, than was Muslim, and Jain, Sindhi and Panjabi were more or less in similar percentage.
- More of the couples were married whereas, for more than thirty years and less twenty two percent were in 20-30 married years.
- Majority of the families had 2-3 children.
- Around 40% of the couples reported to living with their married children in the same house hold.
- Reasons for children living away from parents reported were migration due to education, job and in some cases separation due to lack of adjustments between the two generations.

Adjustment pattern of middle aged couples

- In general there was no significant difference in health, home, social and marital adjustment of middle aged males and females but emotional and financial adjustment of middle-aged males was better than females.

- When compared for difference in adjustment with reference to different demographical variable (Age, education, occupation, age at the time of marriage, family type and married years) it was found that-
- Education came out as one of important factor in adjustment of middle aged couples. It is worthwhile to note that less educated show better health, home, social marital, emotional and financial adjustment than higher education groups. Higher educated males showed better home and emotional adjustment than those educated up to secondary or below.
- It has been observed, that when compared for occupation of couples, working status effects adjustment of males and females. Males in job as well as business category, show better health, home, emotional and financial adjustment than middle aged females. Females in jobs show better health and emotional adjustment as compared to those running their own business.
- Adjustment in middle aged is independent of age at the time of marriage.
- But when compared for married years (duration of marriage) males who were between 21-30 married years show significantly better home and emotional adjustment whereas female in this group reported better health, social, marital and financial adjustment. It seems that there are gradual changes in adjustment pattern as the time passes and in middle age couples for married years thirty or more, no gender differences were noted for various areas of adjustment.
- Home adjustment of joint family females was better than their female counterparts in nuclear families whereas financial adjustment of nuclear family males was better than joint family male respondents

Life satisfaction of middle aged males and females

When compared for life satisfaction, there was no significant difference in life satisfaction for various areas (mental, social, marital and family) except job satisfaction where males showed better job satisfaction than females.

When life satisfaction in different areas of middle aged males and females was compared for their demographic variables, it was found that middle aged males of all age groups showed better job satisfaction than females and social life satisfaction of males in older group was better than females.

- Education emerged as one of the important factor for life satisfaction pattern of middle aged couples. Although males as well females of low education level reported better family satisfaction but it was also noted that higher the education level better the marital, social satisfaction with no gender difference.

  It is also worthwhile to note that at all the education levels job satisfaction of middle aged males was better than their female counterparts and with the increased level of education males reported better job satisfaction within the group also.
- Males in business showed better family life satisfaction than those in service and even better than their female counterparts. It is also true for type of family variable.

Association between adjustment and life satisfaction of husband and wife

- Pearson's correlations calculated for different areas of adjustment scores between husband and wife revealed that there was significant and positive correlation between adjustment of husband and wife. It indicates that low or high adjustment of one spouse may precipitate in low or high adjustment of other pattern. It was also found that all the areas of adjustment are interrelated significantly, and positively which helps to conclude that good or poor adjustment in one area may affect other adjustment areas too.
- Same is true for life satisfaction in various areas since all but one, correlation values are significant and positive.
- For middle aged individuals, life satisfaction is not the result of any one factor but shaped by satisfaction with work, family life, health, conjugal relationships and with well adjustment in all spheres of life. For some individuals, middle age is a time of struggle, for being forced to cope with critical health problems both of self and of parents/ spouse and so metimes siblings and problems with troubled children. Nonetheless adjustment does not necessarily correspond to the life satisfaction so correlations were also calculated for various areas of adjustment with life satisfaction among middle aged males as well as females. Data revealed that -

- Adjustment in various areas (health, home, social, marital, emotional and financial) is significantly and positively related with mental life satisfaction as well as family life satisfaction among middle aged people with no gender difference. Good emotional adjustment is also significant and positively associated with better job satisfaction of middle aged people.
- Correlation of home adjustment and financial adjustment with social life satisfaction is significant but negative indicating that better home adjustment or financial adjustment may lead to less social life satisfaction on vice versa among middle aged males and females. In this age due to over lode of responsibilities couples have to devote more time to family responsibilities, increased financial burden and adjusting family budget to fulfill needs of family members. Middle aged peoples lack time to social life participation and getting along with other which may affect their social life satisfaction.
- But there are, of course, some of the adjustment and life satisfaction in middle age differ by gender, for instance home adjustment negatively affects social and marital satisfaction specially in case of females (as these correlations are negative and significant in case of females but insignificant in case of middle aged males). Trying to meet social responsibility and improve marital satisfaction may take its toll in the form of poor health adjustment.
- Somehow in case of males there was significant but negative correlation between home adjustment and marital satisfaction. Since home adjustment requires a lot of energy, demands, great responsibility leaving no time for conjugal life demand which can influence marital satisfaction in negative manner.

Factors of adjustment and satisfaction in middle adulthood

There are certain factors as perceived by middle aged couples which directly contribute more to negatively influence adjustment and life satisfaction. Findings were as fallows-

Analysis of physical health variables extracted- declining physical strength, huge expenses on medicines, increased dependency on family members, desire to eat peppery and spicy, inability to meet needs of family members.

Mental health- excessive thinking on any issue, inability to keep calm in routine chores, lack of the enthusiasm as earlier, excessive worry, increase in anger, not accepting own mistakes, irritation/ annoyance.

Thinking and decision making- lack of balance in difficult situation, valuing opinion of others, taking quick decision, regret for their own decisions.

Relation with life partner spouse- finding faults of each other, arguing on every issue, highly ambitious, stubborn nature of spouse, nonromantic partner, imposing too many bindings and restrictions, unequal educational status, too lavish or spendthrift or too much stringy attitude.

Family environment, lack of tolerance in the family, frequent arguments and fights in family, rigorous discipline, difference of opinions, lack of harmony, nonemployment of children.

Suggestions

There is increasing interest in the real world applications of research. Some applications, is emerged throughout the research, have been provided in the form of suggestions for mid-age adults, their family member, counsellers for more creative life, strategies to reduce maladjustment and inverse life satisfaction. Finally there are suggestions for further research in the area.

Suggestions for mid age people

- It is important to remain in good health as this factor affects adjustment and life satisfaction. In mid-age people become more susceptible to diseases and other health related issues and expend huge amount on medicines. So it is always better to be financially prepared for worse situations like this by means of saving or insurances.
- Exercise both mind and body on regular basis, regular medical checkups, healthy and well balanced diet help to maintain the level of fitness necessary for an active, independent lifestyle. Physical activity not only provides protection against some diseases (such as coronary heart disease, diabetes, arthritis, hypertension, certain cancers, osteoporosis and depression) , but in addition, ease tension and reduce the amount of stress.
- Mid-adults are recommended to get proper sleep and rest as these are the great rejuvenators. Daily meditation and yoga will increase concentration and diminish worries and anxieties. Good social network, social support, reasonable expectation from youths, use of humor should be some of the important parts of life.

- People should leave worries of office/work in office and should not spoil their relationship at home.
- Good or poor Adjustment of one spouse may lead to good or maladjustment of life partner and even in other family members so being the head of the family, mid-aged couples must learn good diplomacy to keep family members happy and satisfied. Some basic but essential tips of good family diplomacy are: respect emotions of everybody irrespective being younger or elder, spend proper time with family, develop helping and caring nature among family members, and learn how to manage their anger and temperament within and outside family to reduce unnecessary stress and irritation.
- Though being in relationship puts mid age couple in a strong social and emotional bond but being a human being, partner may want their individual space and sufficient freedom in life and actions. People should respect individual desires and likings and respect personal freedom and space of spouse, failing which life partner may develop negative emotions like being dominated or suppressed in your partner's mind causing maladjustment and lacked satisfaction in relationship. Don't try to bound spouse 's reasonable actions and liberties.
- Life satisfaction in mid age is a complex issue that is related to a number of personal characteristic and environmental conditions. Avoid stress by thinking ahead, steadying themselves for the worst that might happen, staying out of the situation one cannot handle and preparing for graceful ageing. Good health, independence, intellectual stimulation, self-fulfillment and friendship are obvious benefits of positive aging.
- In many cases, either one of the spouses dominates the other and spend compromised living with soured relationships. There are many small and seemingly trivial things which play a crucial role in a better happy and harmonious relationship; taking care of each other, mutual respect, good coordination and support, for instance. The couples with vital relationships are most likely to experience continued, positive interactions within marriage.

  Those who enjoy spending time together and can confide in each other usually maintain a close and giving relationship as they age. So mid age couples should devote extra time to spouse to rekindle relationship.

- Include new and challenging activities such as cooking, gardening and even cleaning the house together.
- Sometimes in life when emotionally agitated mid aged, just want someone who patiently listens their problems and let the emotion go on. So give patient listening to partner when in problem and want to share their emotions.
- In middle age family becomes the most important bonding factor for couples. It is something which keeps bonding relationship in ups and downs of the life. People expect their partner to be caring towards the family and provide due respect and attention. This wins the heart of family members, including life partner.
- Being a human being adds positive and negatives in one. Every person has some weaknesses and lacking part. Think and only focus on the good, not the bad in person qualities and characteristics. Not only feeling love toward partner is important, but so is expressing that love. Spending free time with spouse can be one of the best way to revive stalled relationship. Small-small activities like going on morning/evening walk, helping spouse in household work can help to improve marriage bond tremendously. The most desired behavior of the life partner is to standby together when in bad situation and to embrace partner with shortcoming or mistakes (is different from overlooking) and give suggestions and guidance to correct shortcomings without being too critical and judgmental.
- Most of the participants to survey mentioned that the biggest mental health issue they face is, excessive thinking on any issue. 'Inability to control in difficulties', 'excessive worry', 'getting angrier than before', 'irritation / annoyance', etc. These mental health issues can be very much solved, if not completely, by following some creative activities; set new goals, increase personal interests, discover new hobbies, travel, volunteer, devote special time to children and participate in social programs rather than being busy in mundane daily work. This will help to divert mind from problems, and pump in positive thoughts, circulate new hopes and energy and reduce anxiety. It is very essential to be always have something to do, instead of being free. Getting free time enhances futile thinking and unwanted worries.
- Indulgence in vices like chewing tobacco, smoking, drinking does not only degrade health of the person but affect others also. These

activities may further worsen the already degrading health and age related issues and further cause financial problem to the family also. Apart from this, children and upcoming generation also get encouragement to pursue the bad habits which elders of family follow. So abstinence from these activities may help in manifold.

- Parents should take a note of their children's activities, in case they seems suspicious, such as bad company of friends, returning late night, frequently asking for unjustified amounts of money, and keep communication line open.Talking and listening promotes good moral behaviors in family members.
- Middle age can be a time of intellectual discovery and personal growth, exploration of new more realistic choice. They should accept the coexistence of several different point of view and accept their uncertainty, relativism of all options and expecting that different individual work out their own value style.

  Even if they are authority figure of family, opinion of others on many issues are as valued as their own.
- As being the main decision maker of the family, it is important to take all members together. Though it seems small thing but it may help significantly making family bonds strong and develop faith of other members. Sometimes different family members stand on opposite sides of decision and it becomes really very tough to get a common solution. Many a times couples have to sacrifice their own wishes and desires towards greater good of the family.

  Mid-age adults face many transitional phases like mid-age crisis, empty-nest, death of parents, perception of having lesser days to live, and so on, precipitating in very much negative attitude towards life which further exacerbate already not good situation.
- Making decisions in hurry and later feeling remorse on wrong decisions has come out as one of the major problem with mid-age adults. So individual must be poised and consider all aspects of the situation before making a decision. Similarly at this stage many adults highly doubt on their decisions because of judging them on younger and elder generation perspective. It lessen their moral and confidence to take decisions.
- In the survey it came out that life partner being stubborn is one of the most undesirable character. By being stubborn one just not overlooks others point of view but also destroys the bridge for

future suggestions and opinions. Similarly doing altercation on everything is also pointed as very negative feature, by majority of participants. It just not makes relationship with spouse bad, but quarrelsome family environment obstructs mental and psychological growth of children.

- Mid age people should understand that they cannot change every body. So they should be ready to accept people as they are mid - age couples and individuals should understand that they can't change everybody. So they should be ready to accept people as they are. It will reduce conflicts and altercation in family.
- Majority of participants, especially wives reported highly ambitious or stingy partner as one of the most undesirable behaviour overlooking family happiness, similarly being too much miser even after having sufficient prosperity, may result in spoil marital relations.
- Discipline in family is very essential for having a healthy environment and helps members following good habits in all senses. But being too much disciplinarian is equally bad as it makes home as a ring of circus, where every member plays part without emotion and spirit. It makes family relations dull and lifeless. So middle aged should avoid being a strict disciplinarian.
- Children learn from parents, so mid-aged couples should present a role-model for their children in taking and giving due respect and attention to all family members.

Suggestions for family members and children

Children become the source of happiness and bonding factor for the family. In mid-age children are in adolescent age or sometimes are married. Mid-age couple's happiness is based on the attitude and behaviour of their children to a great extent. There are some suggestions for children, which can give higher levels of fulfilment and satisfaction.

- Majority of participants felt, due respect from family members is necessary factor in life satisfaction. Mid-age couples need proper attention also. In case of lack of these two aspects many a times couples feels just an instrument to fulfil needs of younger and elder generation.
- For both mid-age husbands and wives most significant factor in family environment category was children being away from them. This situation can be migration due to job or studies, separation

due to maladjustment in two generations or any other issue. So children living away from home should give frequent visits to mid-age parents, and regularly talk over telephone or by other means. It makes them emotionally satisfied and fulfilled.

- Children should spare time to have casual talks with their parents and listen their experiences and worries.
- Feeling of being understood and loved by family members seems to be integral part of marital satisfaction during mid age. These relationships are difficult in their communication, conflict and unrewarding so family members should devote more time, energy for togetherness.
- They should understand financial, emotional and physiological condition of their parents and should try not to overload them. Additionally, they should spare time to help parents directly or indirectly in their work.
- Children should take care of health of their parents to take food, medicines, physical activities, on time. Children should stop their parents when they are not following proper regimen as per the advice of doctor or suitable to their age and health.
- Children should understand the attitude difference with their parents, due to generation gap or some other factors and try to tolerate occasional interruptions and worries and show proper care and respect to their parents .

Suggestions for old age homes

For some unfortunate mid-age couples who either don't have children or relative to look after them or don't want to stay with their children or whose children don't accept to look after them, old-age homes are the best option. Following are some suggestions for old-age homes to take better care of mid-aged people.

- Keep individuals busy, so that they don't get free time to think about bad things. Recreational activities are best to keep them engaged.
- Diet control, regular exercises and yoga will help mid-age couples keeping up good health.
- Routine medical check-up should be mandatory phenomenon.
- Frequent social interaction and promoting team work will remove the emptiness in their lives.

Suggestion for counsellors

Many mid-aged individuals, who are suffering sour relationship, adjustment and life-satisfaction, either due to their spouse or due to other family members, visit professional-counsellors to get solution for these issues. There are some suggestions for counsellors to help mid-aged couples well.

- Counsellors should keep in mind that mid-aged couples face many transitions like emptynest, sandwiching between young and older generation, financial burdens etc. Due to all these issues it is easy to get irritation and depression.

  Regular exercise, recreational activities and social participation will help them a lot.
- Counsellors should advise mid-aged couples for some saving. Many-a-times financial insecurity can cause deep anxiety and depression.
- Counsellors should also motivate mid-aged couples to spend more time together and help in each-others work.
- If there is some indulgence in vices like tobacco, smoking, gambling or something else, then counsellors should advise to stop it immediately and if necessary provide medical and other de-addiction.

Suggestion for further studies

- Same study can be expanded to larger area for broader generalization.
- Cross cultural and cross sectional researches can be conducted to find out marital satisfaction, stability factors and perception, negative behavior.
- Study on perception of children about middle age can also be conducted to find out impact on marital satisfaction.
- Present research has only been focused on middle aged couples from intact families. It may be considered to study how life event such as death of spouse, divorce, living separately without spouse affect adjustment and life satisfaction during mid age.
- Association between care giving burden for aging parents and stress can also be studied.

- Study can be conducted to find out relationship between differentiation of self and quality of marital relations, adjustment and satisfaction.
- Study can be conducted on empty nest effect and also on its refilling effect.
- Care giving study can also be conducted.
- Only family factors of influence were taken for study but other outside factors can be included.

Bibliography

Alder, E. S. (2010). Age, education level, and length of courtship in relation to marital satisfaction (Master's thesis, Pacific University, 2010). Retrieved from http://commons.pacificu.edu/spp/145

Anderson, T. B., McCulloch, B. J. (1993). Conjugal support: factor structure for older husbands and wives.J Gerontol.,48(3), 133-42.

Atta, M., Adil, A., Shujja, S., & Shakir, S. (2013). Role of trust in marital satisfaction among single and dual-career couples. International Journal of Research Studies in Psychology, 2(4), 53-62.

Ayalon, L., Shiovitz-Ezra, S., Palgi, Y. (2013). Associations of loneliness in older married men and women. Aging & Mental Health, 17(1), 33-9.

Bookwala, J. (2005). The role of marital quality in physical health during the mature years. Journal of Aging and Health, 17(1), 85-104.

Baird, B. M., Lucas, R. E., Donnellan, M. B. (2011). Life satisfaction across the lifespan: findings from two nationally representative panel studies. Social Indicators Research, 99(2), 183–203.

Berg, C. A., Schindler, I., Smith, T. W., Skinner, M., Beveridge, R. M. (2011). Perceptions of the cognitive compensation and interpersonal enjoyment functions of collaboration among middle-aged and older married couples. Psychology and Aging, 26(1), 167-173.

Brockmann, H. (2009). Why are middle-aged people so depressed? evidence from West Germany. German Socio-Economic Panel Study (SOEP) Carstensen, L. L., Gottman, J. M., Levenson, R. W. (1995). Emotional behavior in long-term marriage. Psychology and Aging, 10(1), 140-9.

Clements, R., Swensen, C. H. (2000). Commitment to one's spouse as a predictor of marital quality among older couples. Current Psychology, 19(2), 110-119.

Costa, P. T. Jr, Herbst, J. H., McCrae, R. R., Siegler, I. C. (2000). Personality at midlife: stability, intrinsic maturation, and response to life events. Assessment., 7(4), 365-78.

Crohan, S. E., Antonucci, T. C., Adelmann, P. K., Coleman, L. M. (1989). Job characteristics and well-being at midlife ethnic and gender comparisons. Psychology of Women Quarterly,13, 223–235.

Dabone, Tawiah, K. (2014). Effects of age on marital satisfaction of married people in Sunyani municipality. International Journal of Research in Social Sciences, 3(8).

D'Zurilla, T. J., Maydeu-Olivares, A. and Kant, G. L. (1998). Age and gender differences in social problem-solving ability. Personality and Individual Differences,25(2), 241–252.

Fiori, K. L., Denckla, C. A. (2012). Social support and mental health in middle-aged men and women a multidimensional approach. Journal of Aging and Health, 24(3), 407-438.

Fichten, C. S., Wright, J. (1983). Problem-solving skills in happy and distressed couples: effects of videotape and verbal feedback. Journal of Clinical Psychology, 39(3), 340-52.

Fielder, K. V., Kurpius, S. E. R. (2005). Marriage, stress and menopause: midlife challenges and joys. Psicologia, 19(1-2).

Gaunt, R. (2006). Couple similarity and marital satisfaction: are similar spouses happier. J Pers., 74(5), 1401-20.

Goel, S., Narang, D. K. (2012). Gender differences in marital adjustment, mental health and frustration reactions during middle age. IOSR Journal of Humanities and Social Science,1(3), 42-49.

Goel, S., Narang, D. K., Koradia, K. (2013). Marital adjustment and mental health among bank employees and doctors during middle age (40-55 years) in Delhi. InternationalJournal of Scientific and Research Publications, 3(1), 2250-3153.

Gorchoff, S. M., John, O. P., Helson, R. (2008). Contextualizing change in marital satisfaction during middle age an 18-year longitudinal study.Psychological Science, 19(11), 1194-1200.

Gore, S., Mangione, T. W. (1983). Social roles, sex roles and psychological distress: additive and interactive models of sex differences. Journal of Health and Social Behavior, 24, 300-312.

Hashmi, H. A., Khurshid, M., Hassan, I. (2007). Marital adjustment, stress and depression among working and non-working married women. Internet Journal of Medical Update, 2(1).

Hasani, P. A. M., Mokhtaree, M. R., Sayadi, A. R., Nazer, M. and Mosavi, S. A. (2012). Study of emotional intelligence and marital satisfaction in academic members of Rafsanjan University of medical sciences. Journal of Psychology and Psychotherapy, 2(2).

Hansen, T., Slagsvold, B. Moum, T. (2009). Childlessness and psychological wellbeing in midlife and old age: an examination of parental status effects across a range of outcomes. Social Indicators Research, 94(2), 343-362.

Henry, N. J., Berg, C. A., Smith, T. W., & Florsheim, P. (2007). Positive and negative characteristics of marital interaction and their association with marital satisfaction in middle-aged and older couples. Psychology and aging, 22(3), 428-441.

Helson, R., Soto, C. J. (2005). Up and down in middle age: monotonic and non monotonic changes in roles, status, and personality. Journal of Personality and Social Psychology, 89(2), 194-204.

Hirschberger, G., Srivastava, S., Marsh, P., Cowan, C. P., Cowan, P. A. (2009). Attachment, marital satisfaction, and divorce during the first fifteen years of parenthood.Pers Relatsh., 16(3), 401–420.

Hollist, C. S. and Miller, R. B. (2005). Perceptions of attachment style and marital quality in midlife marriage.Family Relations, 54,46–57.

Huber, C. H., Navarro, R. L.,Womble, M. W., Mumme, F. L. (2010). Family resilience and midlife marital satisfaction. Sage Journals, 19, 63-72.

Isaac, R., Shah, A. (2004). Sex roles and marital adjustment in Indian couples. International Journal of Social Psychiatry, 50(2), 129-41.

Jennifer, A. Volsky, Rushton (1998). Intimacy, Marital Satisfaction, and Sexuality in Mature Couples. (Thesis Concordia University Montréal, QuSbec, Canada) Retrieved from http://www.collectionscanada.gc.ca/obj/s4/f2/dsk2/tape15/PQDD_0003/MQ39 448.pdf

Jan, M. & Masood, T. (2008). An assessment of life satisfaction among women. Studies on Home and Community Science, 2(1), 33-42.

Kasimatis, M. D. and Guastello, D. D. (2012). Parenting style trumps work role in life satisfaction of midlife women. Journal of Articles in Support of the Null Hypothesis, 9(1).

Kashiwagi, K., Hirayama, J. (2003). Marital norm, reality and satisfaction in middleaged couples: why are wives less satisfied than husbands? Shinrigaku Kenkyu. [Article in Japanese], 74(2), 122-30.

Kim, M. (2013). The effect of marital intimacy, sex communication, and sexual satisfaction on the marital satisfaction for Korean middle-aged women. Journal of Next Generation Information Technology (JNIT), 4(8).

Ko, K. J., Berg, C. A., Butner, J., Uchino, B. N., Smith, T. W. (2007). Profiles of successful aging in middle-aged and older adult married couples. Psychology and Aging, 22(4), 705-718.

Kouros, C. D., & Cummings, E. M. (2011). Transactional relations between marital functioning and depressive symptoms. American Journal of Orthopsychiatry, 81(1), 128-138.

Krishna, N., Reddy, M. N., Vranda, Atiq Ahmed, B. P., Nirmala,B., Siddaramu (2010). Work–life balance among married women employees.Indian Journal of Psychological Medicine, 32(2), 112–118.

Lachman, M. E. (2004). Development in midlife. Annu. Rev. Psychol., (55) 305–31.

Lavalekar, A. (2007). Gender wise comparison on emotional intelligence and marital satisfaction. Gender and Behaviour, 5(2), 1388-1405.

Lee, J. E., Zarit, S. H., Rovine, M.J., Birditt, K. S., Fingerman, K. L. (2012). Middleaged couples' exchanges of support with aging parents: patterns and association with marital satisfaction. Gerontology. 58(1), 88-96.

Lehmann, R., Denissen, J. J. A., Allemand, M., Penke, L. (2013). Age and gender differences in motivational manifestations of the big five from age 16 to 60. Developmental Psychology, 49(2), 365–383.

Levenson, R. W., Carstensen, L. L., Gottman, J. M. (1994). The influence of age and gender on affect, physiology, and their interrelations: a study of long-term marriages. Journal of Personality and Social Psychology, 67(1), 56-68.

Li, T. &Fung, H. H. (2012). Partner discrepancies and age differences in marital quality: distinguishing the ideal, expected, and perceived partner.The Journals of Gerontology Series B Psychological Sciences and Social Sciences, 67(4), 417-22.

Moosavi, S. F. (2012). The comparison of family functioning, marital adjustment and intimacy in middle aged and young spouses.

International Research Journal of Applied and Basic Sciences, 3(10), 2015-2021.

Molina, A. S., Klijn, T. P., Delgado, J. B. (2015). Sexual satisfaction in couples in the male and female climacteric stage. Cadernos de Saúde Pública, 31(2).

Momtaz, Y. A., Hamid, T. A., Masud, J., Haron, S. A., Ibrahim, R. (2013). Dyadic effects of attitude toward aging on psychological well-being of older Malaysian couples: an actor–partner interdependence model. Clinical Interventions in Aging, (8), 1413–1420.

Mukhopadhyay, S. (1989). Working status and stress of middle class women of Calcutta. Journal of Biosocial Science, 21(1), 109-14.

Murstein, Bernard, I., Christy, Patricia (1976). Physical attractiveness and marriage adjustment in middle-aged couples. Patricia Journal of Personality and Social Psychology, 34(4), 537-542.

Myers, J. E., & Madathil, J. (2005). Marriage satisfaction and wellness in India and the United States: a preliminary comparison of arranged marriages and marriages of choice. Journal of Counseling & Development, 83(2), 183-190.

Pethtel, O., Chen, Y. (2014). Life regrets and life satisfaction in mature adults. The Journal of Happiness & Well-Being, 2(2), 106-118.

Peterson, J. L., & Miller, C. (1980).Physical attractiveness and marriage adjustment in older American couples. The Journal of Psychology: Interdisciplinary and Applied,105(2), 247-252.

Pinto, M. D. C., & Neto, F. (2012). Satisfaction with sex life among middle-aged adults. International Journal of Developmental and Educational Psychology, 4(1), 463-470.

Rahmani, A., Khoei, E. M., Gholi, L. A. (2009). Sexual satisfaction and its relation to marital happiness in Iranians. Iranian Journal of Public Health, 38(4), 77-82.

Reid, J., &Hardy, M. (1999). Multiple roles and well-being among midlife women: testing role strain and role enhancement theories. Journals of Gerontology. Series B: Psychological Sciences and Social Sciences, 54(6), S329-38.

Reamen, J. I., Agbakala, G., Ako, J. A. (2012). Midlife crisis in the Nigerian family: counseling implication. Journal of Teacher Perspective. Ryan,

L. H., Wan, W. H., Smith, J. (2014). Spousal social support and strain: impacts on health in older couples.Journal of Behavioral Medicine, 7(6), 1108-17.

Saenz, R. (1986). Traditional sex roles, ethnic integration, marital satisfaction, and psychological distress among Chicanas. Retrospective Theses and Dissertations. Paper 8114.

Schmitt, M., Kliegel, M., Shapiro, A. (2007). Marital interaction in middle and old age: a predictor of marital satisfaction? International Journal of Aging & Human Development, 65(4), 283-300.

Seider, B. H., Hirschberger, G., Nelson, K. L., Levenson, R.W. (2009). We can work it out: Age differences in relational pronouns, physiology, and behavior in marital conflict. Psychol Aging, 24(3), 604–613.

Seider, Herschel, B. (2011). Discrete emotion sequences and marital satisfaction in middle-aged and older couples. Dissertation university of California, Berkeley 43 pages Retrieved from http://gradworks.umi.com/34/99/3499356.html

Shek, D. T. L. (1999). Marital quality and health of Chinese couples: a longitudinal study. Journal of Gender, Culture and Health, 4(2), 83-96.

Singh, M., Singh, G. (2005). A study on family and psychosocial health status of middle-aged working women of Varanasi city. The Internet Journal of Third World Medicine, 3(2).

Skowron, Elizabeth, A. (2000). The role of differentiation of self in marital adjustment. Journal of Counseling Psychology, 47(2), 229-237.

Shiota, M. N., Levenson, R. W. (2007). Birds of a feather don't always fly farthest: similarity in big five personality predicts more negative marital satisfaction trajectories in long-term marriages.Psychology and Aging, 22(4), 666–675.

Smith, T. W, Berg, C. A., Florsheim, P., Uchino, B. N., Pearce, G., Hawkins, M., Henry, N. J., Beveridge, R. M., Skinner, M. A., Olsen-Cerny, C. (2009). Conflict and collaboration in middle-aged and older couples: I. age differences in agency and communion during marital interaction. Psychology and Aging, 24(2), 259-273.

Sorensen, P., Cooper, N. J. (2010). Reshaping the family man: a grounded theory study of the meaning of grand fatherhood. Journal of Men's Studies, 18(2), 117-136.

Story, T. N., Berg, C. A., Smith, T. W., Beveridge, R., Henry, N. J., Pearce, G. (2007). Age, marital satisfaction, and optimism as predictors of positive sentiment override in middle-aged and older married couples. Psychology and Aging, 22(4), 719-727.

Suzanne, Degges-White, S. D., & Myers,J. E. (2006). Women at midlife: an exploration of chronological age, subjective age, wellness, and life satisfaction. Adult span Journal. 5(2),67-80.

Vaillant, G. E., Meyer, S. E., Mukamal, K., Soldz, S. (1998). Are social supports in late midlife a cause or a result of successful physical ageing? Indian Journal of Psychological Medicine, 28(5), 1159-68.

Walfisch, S., Maoz, B., Antonovsky, H. (1984). Sexual satisfaction among middleaged couples: correlation with frequency of intercourse and health status.Maturitas., 6(3), 285-96.

White,S.D., Myers, J. E. (2006). Women at Midlife: An Exploration of Chronological Age, Subjective Age, Wellness, and Life Satisfaction. Adultspan Journal, 5(2), 67–80.

Williams, K. (2003). Has the future of marriage arrived? a contemporary examination of gender, marriage, and psychological well-being.J Health Soc Behav.,44(4), 470–487.

Windsor, T. D., Butterworth, P. (2010). Supportive, aversive, ambivalent, and indifferent partner evaluations in midlife and young -old adulthood.Journals of Gerontology. Series B: Psychological Sciences and Social Sciences, 65(3), 287-95.

Yeh, H. C., Lorenz, F. O., Wickrama, K. A., Conger, R. D., Elder, G. H. Jr. (2006). Relationships among sexual satisfaction, marital quality, and marital instability at midlife. Journal of Family Psychology, 20(2), 339-343.

Yuan, J. W., McCarthy, M., Holley, S. R., Levenson, R. W. (2010). Physiological down-regulation and positive emotion in marital interaction. Emotion, 10(4), 467–474.

Zainah, A. Z., Nasir, R., Hashim, R. S., Yusof, N. M. (2012). Effects of demographic variables on marital satisfaction. Asian Social Science, 8(9).

WEBSITES

- https://www.coursehero.com/file/pt87b3/Grandparenting-On-Becoming-a Grandmother-Being-a-Grandfather-Being-a/
- https://www.coursehero.com/file/p1voust/The-decline-in-defined-benefitpensions-and-increased-uncertainty-about-the/
- http://www.msdmanuals.com/professional/geriatrics/social-issues-in-theelderly/religion-and-spirituality-in-the-elderly

Index

A

Adjustment of husband and wife, 65
Adjustment of Middle aged Males and Females, 47
Adjustment pattern of middle aged couples, 78
Age at the time of marriage, 43
Anderson & McCulloch, 14

B

Bangalore, 20
Bem Sex Role Inventory, 20
Better marital adjustment, 20
Bookwala, 20
Brong-Ahafo Region, 27

C

California based study, 25
Career challenges and job satisfaction, 14
Carl Jung, 13
Central India, 34
Chewing tobacco, 84
Chronic disease, 69
Chronic health problems, 20
Chronic marital conflict, 12
Clements & Swensen, 20
Collin's Dictionary, 9

D

Death of a spouse, 11
Demographic factors of emotional adjustment, 54
Demographic factors of family satisfaction, 63
Demographic factors of marital adjustment, 53
Demographic factors of mental satisfaction, 58
Demographic factors of social adjustment, 52
Demographic factors of social satisfaction, 61
Demographic Profile Of Respondents, 41
Doctor couples, 21
Duration of marriage, 79
Dyadic Adjustment Scale, 20

E

Educational background, 15
Emotional adjustment, 12
Erik Erikson, 9

F

Factors of Adjustment and Satisfaction in Middle Adulthood, 36, 41, 69, 81
Family environment, 37, 69, 82
Family life satisfaction, 67
Family members and children, 86
Family relations and adjustment, 12
Family satisfaction, 15
Fielder & Kurpius, 23
Financial adjustment, 78, 81
Financial adjustments, 12

Financial strain, 11
Fiori & Denckla, 30

G

Gastro -intestinal problems, 11
Gender differences, 28
General Background Information Blank, 35
Goel & Narang, 21

H

Hindu religion, 44

I

Individual desires and likings, 83
Intellectual stimulation, 83
Interpersonal relationships, 77
Isaac & Shah, 20

J

Jammu and Kashmir, 25
Jan & Masood, 25
Job satisfaction, 67
Joint family females, 79

K

Kashiwagi & Hirayama, 23
Keep individuals busy, 87

L

Leisure in mid age, 16
Life satisfaction, 13
Life Satisfaction Scale, 36, 78
Life Scale, 26

M

Madhya Pradesh, 34
Madhya Pradesh state, 18
Marital adjustment, 13, 20, 21
Marital intimacy, 27
Marital relationship, 14
Marital relationship and stress, 23
Marital relationship shifts, 10
Marital satisfaction, 11, 14, 27
Marital Satisfaction Scale, 27
Married midlife women, 23
Medical and nutritional benefits, 11
Mental health, 37, 69
Mental satisfaction, 67
Middle adulthood, 9, 14, 78
Middle age couples adjustment, 19
Middle age couples life satisfaction, 22
Middle aged bank employee, 21
Middle aged couples, 18
Middle aged doctors, 22
Middle aged men and women, 69
Middle-age intimacy crisis, 12
Middle-aged adults, 14
Middle-aged challenges, 14
Middle-aged individuals, 24
Midlife mothers, 26
Monthly family income, 44

N

Narsinghpur district, 34, 78
Negative emotions, 83
Non-cooperative behaviour, 75
Non-distressed individuals, 20
Nuclear families, 79
Nuclear family males, 57
Nuclear family system, 44

O

Old Age Adjustment Inventory, 78
Older adult married couples, 29

P

Parental Authority Questionnaire, 26
Personal freedom, 83
Physical attractiveness, 15
Physical disability, 20
Physical illness, 69
Physical symptoms, 20
Poor marital satisfaction, 63
Poorer physical health, 20
Positive and negative affect, 25

Positive thinking and decision making, 37
Post parental years, 75

R

Rafsanjan University of Medical Sciences, 26
Recreational activities, 88
Relation with life partner, 37, 69
Relationships with children, 17
Role of parents and parent-in-laws, 16
Romantic relationship, 22

S

Satisfaction in middle adulthood, 81
Seider & Herschel, 30
Serious illness of spouse, 11
Sex communication, 27
Sexual life, 28
Sexual relations, 17
Sexual satisfaction, 11, 27
Shiota & Levenson, 23
Social and emotional bond, 83
Social satisfaction, 14, 67
Spirituality and adult lives, 16
Sunyani Municipality, 27

T

Terpersonal relationships, 77
Trust Scale, 27
Typical Indian families, 48

U

Unequal educational status, 74
Unhappy marriages, 19
Unsatisfactory relationship, 13
Urbanization and modernization, 17

V

Violent behaviour of spouse, 74

W

White & Myers, 28
Windsor & Butterworth, 15, 29

Y

Young adult group, 28
Young spouses, 21
Younger married people, 28